GOD & GLOBAL JUSTICE:

GOD AND GLOBAL JUSTICE

Religion and Poverty in an Unequal World

EDITED BY
FREDERICK FERRÉ
AND RITA H. MATARAGNON

A NEW ERA BOOK

PARAGON HOUSE
New York

Published in the United States by
Paragon House Publishers
2 Hammarskjold Plaza
New York, NY 10017

A New Ecumenical Research
Association Book

Library of Congress Cataloging in Publication Data

Main entry under title:

God and Global Justice.

(God, The Contemporary Discussion Series)
"A New ERA book."
"A New Ecumenical Research Association book."
Includes index.
1. Church and the poor—Congresses. 2. Distributive justice—Religious aspects—Congresses. 3. Economic development—Religious aspects—Congresses. I. Ferré, Frederick. II. Mataragnon, Rita H., 1947–
III. Series.
BV639.P6G63 1984 291.1′785 84-26538
ISBN 0-913757-36-5 (hardbound)
0-913757-37-3 (paperbound)

Contents

Foreword

The essays in this book will speak plainly enough without editorial assistance, but the history of their origin deserves notice. It is rare when scholars of philosophy, religion, and social sciences from distant places and representing major religions are able to gather. The pocketbooks of most such scholars, especially those from the poorer nations, do not allow the luxury of travel for face-to-face encounters. We tend normally to conduct our dialogues in published journals, which requires a lag time of years between fresh thought and critical rejoinder. Or we read each others' books, kept apart by formality and distance.

This normal unavailability of personal interchange is a significant loss, since thought develops best in spirited give and take, and since understanding—especially across the linguistic and cultural barriers dividing religious thought worlds—is greatly assisted when thinkers can come to know and respect one another personally. Face-to-face dialogue makes it easier to enlarge and improve a position—or catch and remove an error—before it is frozen into permanent print. The isolation of scholars, for want of the means to meet, has been a serious handicap to advancement.

Fortunately for international scholars interested in the study of religion, however, the Unification Church is convinced as a matter of doctrine that it is of urgent and fundamental importance to enhance dialogue among the religions of the world. This conviction has been put into practice through the New Ecumenical Research Association (New ERA), which has sponsored many conferences at which scholars from around the world could for the first time come together in unaccustomed comfort for serious and free exploration of vital topics.

The conference for which the papers in this book were prepared was called God: The Contemporary Discussion. It was held in Puerto Rico from December 30, 1983, to January 4, 1984. In the idyllic setting of the Cerromar Beach Hotel, the philosophers and theologians of our Theme Group, "God and Social Reality," gathered to discuss the gap between such luxury as we were enjoying there and the realities of a world divided between wealth and abject misery. In our group were scholars from Africa and India, North America and South America, Europe and the Philippines; we were Catholic and Protestant, Muslim and Hindu, Unitarian and Unificationist; we were males and females, philosophers and theologians, economists and psychologists, skeptics and priests.

Justice, in the sense of equitable distribution of resources among nations or among members of a society, is certainly not a new topic. Heads of state have discussed global justice and its importance in the attainment of peace. In countless small pockets of the world, religious as well as lay workers have talked of and worked for social justice within their respective communities. On the other hand, academic scholars have been notoriously unresponsive to problems of injustice. Unfortunately, the collective thinking of our modern community of scholars worldwide has yet to make any significant impact on the problem of global justice as it exists today. Thus this group discussion offered an unusual opportunity for interdisciplinary scholars of religion to confront real world problems together. Even if not all presentations or papers yielded concrete or practical action recommendations, awareness and analysis of the many faces of injustice from different perspectives provided valuable insights for better understanding. Despite "tower of Babel" dangers with regard to cultural background, disciplinary perspective, and accustomed methodology, in fact mutual respect and a common interest in the discussion topic made possible fruitful dialogue and professional camaraderie among this small community of scholars.

As it turned out, the participants in our group (co-moderated by the editors, who had previously not met one another) were eager to work at the central question of this volume: whether and how religion can be an important resource for the bringing about of global justice in a world in which poor nations and rich nations currently co-exist without a developed sense of global community and without the institutions that might make for such justice. Of course there were disagreements among us, as will be visible in the chapters that follow. Those disagreements were a large part of the reason for coming together for dialogue. But there was also a fundamental consensus that the spiritual heritage of humanity—

varied as it is—is a potential resource for the deep changes in consciousness that will be requisite for a more humane future.

If this consensus is correct, then our book may be a contribution to the forging of the community among nations and among persons that will lead to the principled relief from suffering that untold numbers pray for daily. No book can expect to change the world by itself; but if our collected contributions—now revised in the light of our discussions and offered as a stimulus for more thought on this great theme—can shake complacency among the rich and offer constructive directions for all concerned, it will have served its purpose and lived up to the hopes of the generous sponsors of our meeting. The world is divided and dangerous in its divisions. Religion, the very word for which was formed from the Latin *religare,* "to bind," may help bind us together in links of mutual concern and responsibility that will lead us back from the brink and turn us away from callous injustice. It is a public resource as well as a private comfort. As such it is too important to be left to theologians alone. In that spirit, we offer our discussions to the world.

FREDERICK FERRÉ, Philosophy
The University of Georgia, Athens, Georgia, U.S.A.

RITA H. MATARAGNON, Psychology
Ateneo de Manila University, Manila, Philippines

Part One
GOD AND THE HUMAN COMMUNITY

1

God and Global Community

FREDERICK FERRÉ

There is at present no global community. The various nations pursue their own advantage, with the rich nations holding most of the power and the poor trying, in various ways (most of them unsuccessful), to achieve a new balance that will be more to their benefit.

In June 1983, in Belgrade, Yugoslavia, we saw the drama played out again at the Sixth United Nations Conference on Trade and Development (UNCTAD VI), where the poorer nations once more tried to persuade the wealthier nations to change the rules and conditions of economic life for a world in which three-quarters of the people have access to a negligible fraction of the earth's material goods. Missing from Belgrade were the earlier strident demands for a "new economic order," which were heard at the 1979 Manila UNCTAD V. In their place were more accommodating requests for short-term adjustments on behalf of the poor. But politeness seems to have no more persuasive power than militancy in a world without the basis of community. The economic recession in the industrial nations gave them an excuse to plead inability and to repeat the refrain "charity begins at home." The Reagan administration almost decided to send no delegation at all to Belgrade, so little attuned are those now in power in the United States to the pleadings and proposals of Third World states.[1]

As we consider "God and Social Reality: The Role of Religion in the Relationship between Rich and Poor Nations," the theme of the meeting that gave rise to this book, it is vital *first,* that we state clearly what undergirding values would need to be acknowledged as necessary conditions for any true global community and, *second,* that we explore what may be contributed in the quest for realizing those necessary conditions by religion.

Global Values

As a starting point for the identification of the fundamental values that will have to be taken into account in any quest for global community—indeed, for any community of human beings of whatever degree of comprehensiveness—we can do no better than reflect on the list of eleven basic values provided by Ian G. Barbour in his recent book *Technology, Environment, and Human Values.*[2] These eleven are divided into three groups, each of which deserve separate attention.

I. Material Values. Barbour offers four values for consideration under this head.

Survival is the value that makes possible all the other values. It is, for the species as for the individual, the sine qua non for the realization of other values. We may wish to note, as Barbour does not, that the survival needs of the individual may not be identical to those of the species. We may also note the fateful irony that a frantic or misguided quest for survival today may be leading the world—in the name of armaments for self-defense—to the very opposite outcome in terrible nuclear destruction. But, such qualifications aside, it is clear that any global community must attend to the real survival needs of its component units, whether these be defined in terms of individual human beings or as subordinate political entities that are themselves ultimately comprised of individual persons.

Health is the material norm that distinguishes mere survival from physically vigorous and wholesome life for individuals or groups. Again, we may wish to add to Barbour's account that modern health technologies, when brought to traditional cultures previously lacking in such technologies, have had a double-edged effect on the well-being of such cultures. Infant mortality has been dramatically reduced by public health practices, and the individual tragedies of death by cholera and the like have been greatly reduced. At the same time, however, the intervention of such novel health technologies has been one of the main causes of the awful burden of overpopulation that keeps the yoke of poverty on the necks of the developing countries. Such ironies, however, do not detract from the reality that health for individuals and for populations (again, not always quite the same thing) is a value to be sought for any biotic community, including the global community we seek.

Material welfare is desirable as well as health, and often health will clearly depend upon at least a minimal level of material wealth.

As Barbour puts it: "Beyond survival and health, people seek a higher level of material well-being, including housing, transportation, and a variety of goods and services."[3] Often, of course, material welfare will depend upon the health of an individual or group; e.g., one of the motives for school breakfast programs in the United States was concern that adequate nutrition be assured to the disadvantaged so that the weary cycle of poverty might at last be broken. On the other hand, the value of material welfare might be a trap, unless we are careful about placing it in context, since by itself it seems to have no limit or optimum, and it may well be that one of the obstacles to genuine community at neighborhood or national as well as at global levels is the unbalanced attention of individuals and groups to this value. In its proper place, however, and in connection with other values, material welfare is surely a value that should be acknowledged as necessary for global community.

Employment is the final item on Barbour's list of material values. In some ways it is an obvious and appropriate addition to the list. For many it provides the primary access to material welfare through income earned. At the same time, health and some minimum level of material well-being (access to tools, transportation, etc.) provide the necessary conditions in many societies to employment. Above all, the question of "jobs" certainly represents a major value issue in many public policy decisions. On the other hand, the employment value is less universal than the others we have considered so far. It is more bound to particular societies and economies than are the values of survival, health, and material welfare. Perhaps a global community could be founded without a commitment to the value of employment in the sense normally used in the industrial world. Perhaps commitment to the value of material welfare is all that is required at such an ecumenical level. Still, what is represented by "employment" in Barbour's list is hardly optional, especially if this value is understood not only in terms of material welfare, but also, as E. F. Schumacher points out,[4] in terms of creative expression, dignity, solidarity with community well-being, and just distribution of social benefits and responsibilities. But with these considerations we have already left the material for the social dimension. Employment remains an ambiguous category, then, and should be handled with care in any listing of value requirements for the global community. Perhaps it would be best, therefore, to distribute it under the various headings, material and social, where its genuine force is felt.

We are left, after this critique, then, with three vital material conditions for any value scheme aiming to ground global community: such a scheme must have a way of attending to the survival, health, and material welfare needs of those to be included in the universal community. These attentions, however, as we have seen, must be guarded against the ironies and excesses that material values, alone regarded, may involve. One of the guarding dimensions, next to be considered, is that of social values.

II. Social Values. Barbour offers four more values under this head, and although he does not take explicit notice of their internal relationships within the social dimension, they may in fact be seen as standing in interesting dialectical tension with one another.

Distributive justice must be a primary concern in any normative community. Merely piling up a total of good things, like health or material well-being, is not enough; a genuine community will also be concerned about how those good things are distributed among its members. If most of the goods go to a relative few, for example, and many are left with mere crumbs from the banquet of others, then real community must feel the injustice and have means of redressing the imbalance. Indeed, even if the "greatest number" are happy at the expense of an oppressed or disadvantaged minority, the claims of justice should continue to disturb the complacent majority until this essential value is restored. In a global community this would mean that no nation could fatten itself in good conscience while others starved; more, it would mean that mechanisms in defense of justice would need to exist in such a community so that unjust distribution could not permanently perpetuate itself in the international system. Not only between nations, but also between generations—the living and those not yet born—would justice be required in a real community spanning not only global space, but significant human time. The present generation would need to accept limits on its own well-being if these should be necessary to prevent the inequitable shifting of burdens to successor generations.

Participatory freedom, on the other hand, is of vital social value in any community that preserves the sense of dignity and responsibility of its individual members. There must be controls for the sake of justice, but such controls run against the values of freedom—unless such controls are acknowledged as just and are adopted with the full participation and consent of those whose actions are to be controlled. Without such a sense of personal participation, the individual loses his or her sense of agency and the creative powers of hope.[5] Thus we face the dialectical task of envisioning a global community in which the values of freedom are not trampled by the demands of justice, but, conversely, freedom is not defined as individual license against the just needs of community. Only an enlarged horizon of awareness in the general population, grounding an attitude of consent in just limitations, would seem to provide a possible solution to this conflict of basic values.

Interpersonal community is a value stressed by Barbour as frequently broken in modern times, especially by the advance of technology: "Often community cohesion has been sacrificed to other values. An urban freeway cuts through an ethnic neighborhood and pollutes its air—for the benefit of suburban commuters. Developing countries experience the breakdown of cultural traditions and social solidarity when Western technologies are imported."[6] The needs of human beings for other human beings in appropriately scaled, mutually sustaining relationships must be recognized in any larger, global community.

Personal fulfillment is not to be forgotten, however, in the emphasis on community. Nor is it to be identified, as it often is, with possessions. What really fulfills persons needs to be the sustained concern of all who care for viable global community. Again this may smack of dialectical tension, since relational interests may seem to be at odds with individual goals. But a broadening awareness of the extent to which personal fulfillment actually depends upon supporting interpersonal relationships, and of the degree to which healthy community requires fulfilled individuals in voluntary interaction, may be able to overcome the apparent tension.

Barbour's list of four social values, then, relate in polar tensions: justice strains against freedom just as community pulls against personal fulfillment. We might, indeed, reduce his list of four social values to only two great ones, since distributive justice might be subsumed under the requirements of community, and participatory freedom might be subordinated to the needs of autonomous fulfillment. But in either case, the answer to the tensions that have led historically to excesses in either direction—to those oppressive communities in which totalitarian directives neglect the fulfillment of individuals and, conversely, to those atomistic societies in which selfish individualism overwhelms social conscience—may be overcome only by a new consciousness: of the genuine need of the complete individual for relationship and of the community for fulfilled persons. So far, however, the only values we have noted are distinctly anthropocentric. These may, indeed, serve to balance excessive preoccupation with material values; but if we are to hope for truly global community, must we not admit values that balance an excessively narrow or shortsighted preoccupation with our species alone? The final trio of environmental values will redress such an imbalance.

III. Environmental values. Not all traditional ethical positions have made explicit place for values that are not exhaustively reducible to human needs. Barbour, however, moves carefully but decisively into this new dimension.

Resource sustainability is a clear value for any community that cares about its transgenerational time span. The greater the extent to which the current generation is able to live off renewable resources rather than plundering the earth of its capital stores, the better for intergenerational justice. Current economic thinking, political calculation, and technological practice all tend, as Barbour points out, to be oriented almost exclusively toward short-run costs and benefits. A responsible global community will need to be grounded in a reformed awareness of the needs of the long run and the possibilities of living better within our income.

Ecosystem integrity is a value that begins the transition to concern beyond even the long-run benefits of the human species. At one level, of course, it can be argued that a healthy ecosystem is the surest guarantee of a benevolent environment for man. Much evidence, indeed, shows that ecological diversity is the secret of ecological stability, and that the enlightened self-interest of the human species lies in the direction of self-restraint when our short-term wants conflict with the fragile web of life around us. At another level, however, it is also possible to insist that our obligations run beyond even our own species' interests to the fundamental needs of life itself. We are a small part of life, but we are endowed with powers that could conceivably destroy life on the one planet where life is known to exist. Do we not have a profound obligation to honor the larger life we share, even if it requires that we forswear the use of all such ultimate weapons for the sake of the common biotic good? If this is clearly true on the largest scale, where extinction of all life is at issue, then is it not also to some degree true as well in lesser cases, where endangered species depend upon our self-restraint for their existence? Even if it is not the case, then, that human enlightened self-interest can be shown to lead to policies in support of the integrity of the ecosystem, these policies are to be valued by the global community.

Environmental preservation leads one further step to concern for the earth's integrity even beyond the biotic level. Barbour's treatment of it mainly stresses the importance of pure air, water, and land for human health and human aesthetic enjoyment—and these are among the clear reasons to value the preservation of our total environment. But, in addition, we may wish to see the global community founded upon a recognition of the dignity of nature in itself, with which the human community may interact in creative and fruitful ways, but which is never to be conceived merely as resource pit and garbage dump.

Distributive justice, then, no less than the legitimate quest for material welfare, may demand that human needs be urgently met by the intense exploitation of the earth; but neither material nor social values should be given full sway in the ideal global community without consideration of the environmental values that undergird our human intercourse with the planet itself. As Barbour puts it, "I am particularly concerned about ways of combining environmental preservation and distributive justice. This double goal has been called ecojustice. The gap between humanity and nature and the gap between rich and poor are equally serious."[7]

Thus we conclude our list of the basic values on which our global community should be built: *survival, health, material welfare; interpersonal and personal fulfillment; ecojustice.* Is there a role for religion, broadly conceived, in providing the conditions in consciousness that such a set of values and such a global community will require?

The Role of Religion

Since religion most essentially exists in that molten dimension where occur the most intense and comprehensive valuations of individuals or groups—the dimension of the sacred[8]—our question should not be whether there is a role for religion in influencing the value-laden conditions that alone could allow the emergence of true global community. Religion, after all, constitutes the very cauldron of value from which the motivational power for any pattern of life, whether parochial or ecumenical, must be dipped. Religion as the expression of fundamental value perceptions must inevitably have a role in any fundamental value change. The question, therefore, should be whether the religions of the world give promise of providing the power needed in our day to transform parochial consciousness into global. Are the world's religious resources well suited to the value requirements that we have laid out for a just and sustainable world community?

The scope of our question is too broad for properly nuanced treatment in a brief chapter such as this. Ideally, the scholarly task would be to sift through the evidence and find those respects in which the answer could be positive, distinguishing these carefully from the other respects in which a negative conclusion might be drawn. Then the different respects would need to be weighed to determine whether the positive resources could be separated from the negative and whether, on balance, the religious tradition under consideration could be deployed, with others, in the service of our historic need. Perhaps just such a sustained and systematic study could be one useful long-term result of a series of conferences, like the conference that gave rise to this book, made up of scholars from all the major religious traditions of the world. The quick survey of the main valuational lines of the funded religious wisdom of the ages, which follows, suggests that there is much to be hoped from such a sustained enterprise.

Religious Traditions and the Wisdom of the Ages. The human race has never been without some religious expression of basic values, and material values are not alien to the fundamental religious phenomenon. The old religion of ancient Egypt, the worship of Amon, emerges, like the civilization it undergirds, out of the realities of life along the Nile. The birds, the beetles, the crocodiles, the papyrus reeds of the region—all provided the earthly content for sacred symbols only half detached from the rich earth of the river valley that offered its inhabitants survival, health, and material well-being. In Greece the pipes of Pan wove pagan harmonies around the rocky landscape in which trees and streams were felt to be inhabited by wood nymphs and water sprites. Mundane economic activities such as fuel gathering or fishing could not occur outside the sacred context. Native American religion, long before the coming of the Europeans, expressed the piety of religious valuation in the face of the exigencies of survival, such as the need for rain or the necessities of the hunt. The Indian hunter's prayer of apology to the prey he needs to kill for survival is by now well known and seems strange to some.[9] It is, however, not spiritually alien to the impulse, seemingly universal among us, to give thankful recognition in ceremonial ways—often through stylized prayer—for daily food. The custom of saying or singing grace before (and sometimes after) meals is a deep reminder of the affirmative place that many religions have for the material values. There is indeed ground in the wisdom of the ages for a humble common recognition of the material context in which all human beings, the world over, find themselves, and therefore of the validity of the values that survival, health, and material welfare represent.

Religions have, however, traditionally put these material values into the needed context of other, normally supervening, values of personal or interpersonal fulfillment. Islam, although it finds the pursuit of material values entirely legitimate, reminds all Muslims that they are under a higher, sacred authority. Every activity—economic, political, or social—stands subject to the will of Allah. Judaism and Christianity provide the same sort of context for the material values that they sanction and bless, as in harvest festival and marriage ceremony. God is to be praised in the breaking of bread, but man does not live by bread alone. The tendency within the biblical religions, indeed, is to express in various ways not only this dialectic between material and social values, but also the bipolarity we noted earlier between the demands of interpersonal fulfillment (justice, community values) and personal fulfillment (freedom, individual values). Different subtraditions within the same religion, indeed, may stress different poles of this duality. Protestantism has in general stressed the personal values of responsible selfhood, whereas Catholicism has maintained more centrally a corporate sense and pointed up the essentially social character of human fulfillment. Still, neither has let go entirely of the other side of the polarity: with few exceptions, Protestant Christians maintain a doctrine of the church and Christian fellowship in salvation, just as Catholic Christians remember the individual sinner and saint in the midst of community. In the religious traditions of millions of persons today there are clearly resources for the dynamic balancing of material with social values and community with individual values on a global scale, if only these can be constructively related to one another and deployed in the service of the emergent global community.

What, though of the environmental restraints that we saw also to be needed for the long-run health of the global community? Christianity and Judaism have been accused of encouraging the heedless exploitation of the planet.[10] This charge has been extensively discussed,[11] and the verdict in general has been that these religions are open to abuses of this sort, but that within them are countervailing values that make the earlier charges simplistic. Even more obvious, however, are the environmental restraints implicit in other religions of the world that might complement the biblical religions in this respect and reinforce the nonexploitative aspects of biblical teaching. Buddhism's fundamental sense of harmony with nature may, for example, be expressed through the concrete imagery of the Chinese garden's beautiful proportions and, ideally, its melting of the distinctions between natural and artificial. The human race finds itself within nature as part of it and acts to perfect the tendencies already there. The stress in Hinduism, as well, on the oneness of all things with Brahma, on the eternal transformative dance with Shiva (or Kali) in which destruction and rebirth are mingled, or on the many manifestations of Vishnu, reinforce the sense of sacred kinship among all existences within the apparent world. Taoism, too, stresses the power of nonaction, countering the excessive tendency toward human engineering of nature with a respect for the ultimate counterforces and equilibria at the heart of reality. This is not to say that similar strands of perception are not to be found in other religions, including the biblical religions (note, for instance, the appearance of Saint Francis), or that the material values are wholly neglected in the oriental religions (recall the earthly concerns within Confucianism); but letting the pendulum swing to the East on this dimension may provide helpful counterbalance to the typical consciousness of the West as we look to a global community where West and East are both transcended in a new whole containing, but greater than, all its parts.

Polymythic Organicism and the Wisdom of Life. If it is true that the religions of the world, variously considered, have among them the valuational resources to support the material, social, and environmental values that are essential to the nurture of true global community, then to what extent can we hope (1) that these values can be melded into a complementary unity despite the vast differences between specific traditions, and (2) that this universal valuational framework, if achieved, can motivate persons to care inclusively rather than parochially about other persons in distant lands and remote generations? Only if both these conditions are met, it would seem, can the positive influence of religion play an effective role in transforming global community from a lofty ideal into actual historic reality.

Organicism is the term that can be applied to the position holding that our fundamental ethical choices should be guided by the wisdom of life, as seen in healthy living organisms or societies of organisms. The leading philosophers of organicism who have influenced the following account are H. Bergson and A. N. Whitehead, though the argument that follows is not intended as a recital of either's explicit doctrine.[12]

Every healthy organism manifests three great principles in dynamic tension: the principle of creativity, the principle of homeostasis, and the principle of holism. Life is creative. Life is conservative. Life is integral. One of the most noteworthy facts about living things is their tendency to grow and to reproduce and to spread into all available "niches." This is the reality of the principle of creativity; but creativity alone and unchecked—like cancer—would be destructive, both at the level of the individual organism and at the level of the society. Healthy life therefore has built-in mechanisms that balance creativity with constraint. Homeostatic controls prevent gigantism and maintain balance within the organism, just as analogous controls of various sorts in most species prevent population overshoot and subsequent collapse. This principle of homeostasis, however, is made possible only by the intricate set of connections and feedback loops within living organisms that make the creative-constrained entity a genuine whole.

The value system derived from the wisdom of life would stress, for human existence, the creative growth and material health and well-being that is a part of all flourishing biotic existence. But it would stress, as well, that such growth must be placed within internally regulated limits to avoid the dangers of distorted development or overgrowth and collapse. These limits would be grounded in a constant flow of communication among the differentiated parts of human society, with mutual adjustment among the parts for their maximal well-being to assure the well-being of the whole. In other words, organicism would support all the material values and the social value of participatory freedom on the basis of the principle of creativity; it would support the social value of distributive justice on the basis of the principle of homeostasis; and it would support ecojustice on the basis of the principle of holism.

These, of course, are the values necessary for global community. They are also the values that are variously supported by religious wisdom of the ages. Since this is so, might it not be hoped that the literal content of organicism, a philosophy and moral code based on the general understanding of the wisdom of life, could be agreed on as a common core underlying and interpreting the more specific mythic elaborations offered by the various religions of the world? All developed religions can be seen to have a mythic, imagistic element and a theoretical, explicative element.[13] If organicism could be accepted as a common denominator (not, of course, as the whole scheme, but as an integral part) within all the explicative schemes of the religions of the world, then the basis for a responsible ecumenism, as solid as life itself, would be laid. The individual religions would retain what William James called their specific "over-beliefs,"[14] but these would be differences within a context of consensus on just those values that would ground them and their adherents in a nascent global community. The basis of global community, then, is organicism tolerant of and open to explication in terms of a variety of mythic images. Such may be called *polymythic organicism,* by virtue of its hospitality to various religious embodiments in culturally relevant, historically venerated mythic images. Polymythic organicism is the foundation needed for a coherent religious role in the founding of global community.

What real prospect, however, is there that the religions of the world, even if united on the principles of polymythic organicism, will in fact be able not only to raise the consciousness of their throngs of adherents to the universal applicability of these values, but also to motivate them to behavior in accordance with the universal scope of global need? The theoretical issue is not a major obstacle, since the universality of moral considerability is built into the very foundations of polymythic organicism itself: all life is considerable, no man or nation is an island in a holistic framework. But the practical issue is difficult to answer with any confidence. This is so because it is dependent upon forces not under human control.

Whence comes the power of religion to motivate? Some might answer in terms of the wisdom of life, something akin to the *élan vital* of Bergson, perhaps; and this might be enough for our answer. If life is threatened, as never before, by national divisions and parochial rivalries, perhaps the wisdom of life will speak with power through religious images that could bind all people together, also as never before, into a life-defending global community. Others might answer more specifically in terms of the particular images of their traditions and call upon God. Kathleen Dugan, in chapter 4 of this book, deals stimulatingly and at greater length with this question in terms of the psychology and the spirituality of "conversion" that entails an essential social and ethical dimension. Whether it be God, or Jungian archetypes, or the wisdom and power of life to save itself, we may perhaps never know. What we do know is that the world requires justice and that justice, to be effective, requires the consciousness of community. Scholars may find the theoretical basis for such community in religion, but scholars cannot hope to engineer the general reform in human consciousness that is needed to meet our critical moment. Let us do what we as scholars can do, then, and sweep away the gratuitous obstacles to ecumenical support of world consciousness. Then let us live gently on the earth, supporting the germination of global community wherever possible, and finally trusting in life, or God, for the final outcome.

NOTES

1. David Winder, "The Poor Nations' Hollow Truce with the Rich," *Christian Science Monitor,* June 9, 1983.
2. Ian G. Barbour, *Technology, Environment, and Human Values* (New York: Praeger, 1980), chap. 1.
3. Ibid., 3.
4. E. F. Schumacher, *Small Is Beautiful: Economics as if People Mattered* (New York: Harper & Row, 1973), chap. 4.
5. Erich Fromm, *The Revolution of Hope: Toward a Humanized Technology* (New York: Bantam Books, 1968).
6. Barbour, ibid., 4–5.
7. Ibid., 6.
8. Frederick Ferré, *Basic Modern Philosophy of Religion* (New York: Scribner's, 1967), chaps. 3 and 4.
9. John Neihardt, *Black Elk Speaks* (Lincoln, Nebraska: University of Nebraska Press, 1961).
10. Lynn White, Jr., "The Historical Roots of Our Ecologic Crisis," *Science* 155 (1967).

11. David and Eileen Spring, eds., *Ecology and Religion in History* (New York: Harper & Row, 1974).
12. Frederick Ferré, *Shaping the Future* (New York: Harper & Row, 1976), especially chaps. 5–9.
13. Ferré, *Basic Modern Philosophy of Religion,* especially chaps. 12 and 13.
14. William James, *The Variety of Religious Experience: A Study in Human Nature* (New York: Longman, Green, and Co., 1902), chap. 20 and especially 513ff.

2

Power, Peace, and the Possibility of Survival

RITA NAKASHIMA BROCK

The world faces an increasing disparity in the economic development of rich and poor nations. At the same time, it faces an increasing arms race as the wealthier nations develop and stockpile weapons of destruction in an attempt to guarantee safety. The U. S. Government policy of "deterrence" is used to keep war at bay by intimidating the enemy and increasing the threatening capabilities of U.S. weapons systems. Ideological wars are then exported to poorer countries, such as Vietnam, where war can continue without damage to wealthier nations.

The lengthening shadow of the threat of a nuclear cataclysm has fueled the peace movements of North America and Europe. The existence of increasingly complex nuclear weapons appears to make war unthinkable. But the question emerges of how war can be made unthinkable. The balance-of-powers solution settles for a tit-for-tat stalemate of stockpiled weapons, a solution designed to be ready for war to protect ideologically controlled territories. Such a stalemate is not peace, as poorer countries that have become battlegrounds can attest.

Death by Competition

The problem with the balance-of-powers solution and the attempt to reach a standoff by deterrence is that the balance itself is not a stable process, and the continual need to rebalance imbalances produces the arms race. *The arms race kills, even without war.*[1] Hence, the race itself destroys us, even as it claims to protect peace. The death-delivering capacity of the arms-race system lies not in its weapons, but in the race itself. This capacity is nowhere more evident than in the growing disparity between the rich nations that make, stockpile, and sell weapons to allies and the poor nations that struggle to meet basic human needs for hundreds of millions of people while being forced to purchase weapons. The arms race also kills the poor within rich nations, for example in the United States, where hunger and poverty have increased because of federal spending cuts in human services and increases in defense spending, while the Reagan administration declares hunger does not exist. In addition, the arms race kills those, especially in the Pacific Islands, whose homelands have become testing grounds for new weapons.[2]

The arms race affects the distribution of resources at a global level. The world in 1979 spent about $16,000 per soldier and about $260 educating a child. To put it another way, what the world spends on weapons in about two and a half weeks would provide basic human needs—food, housing, education, and health care—for the entire human population.[3] Meanwhile, the superpowers sell, not food, but protection to Third World countries, expanding the network of intimidation and insecurity. The world's children are sacrificed to starvation at the rate of one child under two years of age per minute.[4]

The arms race kills more, however, than the world's children and Pacific Islanders. It kills our ability to care by deceiving us into thinking that the competitive race will deliver peace of mind even as we concretely experience insecurity and fear. The arms race is an endless competition and it kills our spirit of hope and caring. It teaches us to fear others and want to control them, and it teaches us that this control is more important than feeding the hungry and liberating the oppressed.

The prophet Isaiah in the Hebrew Scriptures said it well when he claimed the only way to end war and bring peace with justice was to turn weapons into instruments of food production and to stop the study of war altogether (Isa. 2:4), else injustice would continue to produce the curse of endless war. But to end the arms race requires at least three major changes: systemic changes in the way the world's economy operates; a change in U.S. military and foreign-aid policies; and a major change in how we see things so that the insanity of the arms race will be made clearly visible.[5]

This chapter addresses itself to the last of these changes, to an alternative way of seeing and living that challenges conventional understandings of power, especially as power is understood within Western culture and Christian theology. This alternative view of power and the identity structures that produce the new vision of power are drawn from feminism. Philosophical explanations that help clarify the new view of power are drawn from process/relational thought, which bases itself in a metaphysics that helps to make feminist insights clearer conceptually.

The nonsubstance-oriented metaphysics of process/relational thought can be found in parallel forms in other traditions, for example in Buddhism.[6] Yet Buddhist cultures have had their share of war and militarism, and they too, like the West, are male-dominated cultures. Hence, feminism is a major key to this shift in understandings of power. It is within the identity structures and actual worlds of women that an alternative view of power is lived. The fact that the public world of politics and policies that engenders the arms race is male dominated is significant, and the virtual global exclusion of women from decision-making public spheres has now endangered the entire planet.

Feminism, in its nineteenth-century arguments for peace, claimed that women's socialized differences from men led to a less violent nature, but also to a more acquiescent and less activist nature.[7] Recent research by feminists on female identity seems to confirm the earlier intuition that women are different and that the difference is crucial. The results of feminist research on the content of that difference indicates that Christian theology is still dominated by male perceptions of identity and power and continues to rely on an intellectual tradition that is almost entirely masculine. This constitutes a rather complex problem in the search for theologies that do not share the same basic presuppositions about reality and power that lead to war. The active exclusion of women appears now to have placed much of theology also within the mind-set that threatens our species and perhaps all of creation.

It is not my contention in this essay that differing perceptions of power in males and females are biologically predetermined or that such perceptions cannot be changed. Rather, my contention is that the institutions of patriarchy that oppress women and divide society into gender-linked roles and value systems produce the difficulty we face because they produce the differing views of power. Men reproduce the divergence in institutions when they exclude women from full participation at every level of society and assume that the masculine view of reality is all-inclusive.

This essay will compare Western male views of identity and power with female views and the implications of those views for Christian theology. Feminist psychology and literature have been selected for their ability to articulate and use traditional female experience in creating an alternative picture of the self and power. Process/relational theology has been selected because its alternative metaphysics seems more akin to feminist ideas than other forms of theology and presents an alternative to a typically masculine view. It also illustrates the point made above that these views are not essentially gender-linked or unchangeable.

The two fields together, process and feminism, present a view of identity and power that raises serious questions about the doctrines of traditional theology. The two fields present a way toward a life-giving theology that questions the presuppositions of war and oppression.

The Power that Delivers Death

Feminist criticism of the oppression of women names the power that delivers death patriarchal power. Feminist examinations of the patriarchal worldview have focused especially on the issues of hierarchy and dualism. Susan Griffin in "The Way of All Ideology"[8] and *Pornography and Silence: Culture's Revenge Against Nature* critically examines the paradigm of conflict and struggle that involves either/or decisions based on a dualistic polarization of opposites. Hierarchies of being become grounded in valuation in favor of one side of a dualism. The paradigm disconnects relationships through competition. It fosters divisions by creating enemies through false allegiances to abstract ideologies. Griffin's term for patriarchy is the "pornographic mind." It traffics in absolutes by repressing aspects of itself that do not yield power and control.

The pornographic mind, motivated by fear, races toward self-destruction by lying to itself about what it destroys. This mind is fueled by fear of itself as a vulnerable creature. The pornographic mind represses what it fears by denying its own inner yearnings and projecting what it fears upon others. It claims for itself such things as transcendence, light, goodness, and changelessness and projects onto the other evil, darkness, sensuality, and unreliability. The mind then controls or destroys the "others," whom it fears because they remind it of its own vulnerability. Thus the pornographic mind races to destroy our fullest connectedness to self, to nature, and to others.

It is no accident that within patriarchy women have been the "other" and have been closely tied to nature, whereas men have been truly "human" and transcend nature. Simone de Beauvoir's

The Second Sex and Susan Griffin's *Women and Nature: The Roaring Inside Her* are comprehensive feminist examinations of the patriarchal attempt to objectify and use women. They show how the oppression of women is deeply embedded in the worldview and institutions of Western culture.

Nancy Chodorow's *The Reproduction of Mothering: Psychoanalysis and the Sociology of Gender* and Carol Gilligan's *In a Different Voice: Psychological Theory and Women's Development* provide important clues to understanding why women have been so objectified and used and why patriarchal power has dominated the Western historical experience. Chodorow's work examines the question from the perspective of observed differences in male and female identity formation and the resulting notions of selfhood. Gilligan contrasts divergent understandings of the self and power in males and females that result in differences in ethical decision making.

Chodorow observes that one of the few universal and enduring elements where there is a sexual division of labor is that women in families are responsible for the primary care of infants and children. Fathers rarely take the role of primary nurturer. Because the family is *the* personal sphere of society, the "quintessentially relational and personal institution,"[9] it is the arena that prepares and then supports individuals in their societal attitudes and roles. Although most societies assume this division of labor is natural and inevitable, Chodorow believes it lies at the heart of the problem of patriarchy. It is the family that provides the core of any society's sex-gender system and is therefore implicated in "the construction and reproduction of male dominance itself."[10]

Using the research of psychologists and sociologists, as well as the data of past psychoanalytic research, Chodorow develops a theory of development and identity formation that highlights the differing perceptions of the self in men and women. She believes the difference develops because of parenting patterns, rather than because of biology, and that therefore there is nothing predetermined about male self-identity and the need for dominance or female self-identity and the tendency toward submission.

Male identity, with its concern for masculinity, according to Chodorow, develops differently from female identity because others are nearly always the primary nurturers. Masculinity becomes an issue precisely because it is less available and accessible to the child. Masculinity becomes idealized and represents dominance in the larger society. Femininity comes to represent regression and lack of autonomy so that masculine maturity rests in denying or repressing attachment and identification with the mother. Thus, boys develop feelings of masculinity largely in negative terms through a strong emphasis on individuation and a more defensive firming of experienced ego boundaries. "Given that masculinity is so elusive, it becomes important for masculine identity that certain social activities are defined as masculine and superior, and that women are believed unable to do many of the things defined as socially important"[11]

Male identity is based on differentiation from others, on generalized, abstract categories defining the masculine roles, and on rejection of femininity and denial of affective relation. The male self is categorized as apart from relationships and affiliation.

Accompanying this masculine identity founded on autonomy and a more rigid role-identified ego boundary is a concept of power closely tied to the notion of an isolated self. Carol Gilligan cites research by David McClelland in *Power: The Inner Experience* that describes the male experience of power as something a self gains, drawing more and more to the self and using the acquired power to gain more over and against others who threaten the self's power. Involvement with others is tied to a qualification of power and identity. The pattern of power perceived internally by males is an ascending thrust toward a transcendental aim, a need to rise and narrow upward toward a hierarchical peak of strength from which all else can be controlled. This power is manifested in the self through assertion and aggression. Inequality in relationships is perceived as a permanent state in which power cements domination and subordination. The extent of the possession of such power is the primary measure of self-worth.

From her research on male identity formation and masculine views of power, Gilligan concludes in her study that male ethical decision making focuses on the balancing of unilateral powers with an emphasis on abstract rights. The need for a balance of powers bases fairness and justice on making separations and distinctions among independent selves.

Bernard Loomer in his essay "Two Conceptions of Power" calls patriarchal power unilateral power.[12] Unilateral power presupposes an ego-centered, substantialist view of the self and understands a powerful self as one that aims at creating the largest determining effect on others while being minimally influenced by others. Unilateral power is grounded in competing claims for power and either/

or choices, presupposing that when one self gains power another has less. Others exist ambiguously as positive means to the enhancement of a self's power or as negative obstacles to the exercise of a self's power. The self values itself on the strength of its unilateral power. "In our struggle for greater power it is essential that the other be as restricted as possible, or that the freedom of the other be contained within the limits of our control—whether the other be another person or group or the forces of nature. We hesitate or refuse to commit ourselves to those people or realities we cannot control."[13]

In this unilateral understanding of power, conflict and competition are the basic paradigms of interaction; and value is structured hierarchically. Worth is measured by winning more power. Those with less power have less claim upon life and resources. Only when an oppressed group competes for power and gains a sufficient amount to force those over them to negotiate does it merit consideration for protection or an equitable share of resources. Those who can safely be ignored are trampled under. To keep the threat of other powers under control the emphasis is on overinflating the extent of the possession of unilateral power. The more one appears to have power, the more value and respect one is accorded.

Repression of aspects of the self and oppression of others are hallmarks of unilateral power. Aspects of the self that threaten its control and independence must be denied. Those capacities and concerns that enhance the specialized interests of unilateral power are abstracted from a full and complete relationship with the self. Similarly, relationships with others and the external world focus on abstracting those elements relevant to the purposes of unilateral power.

> Our interest in others is highly selective. We are not concerned to deal with the full concrete being of the other—whether the other be a person or nature in its livingness or God . . . we . . . shape ourselves in accordance with our own ethical projections, and thereby maintain both our independence and the feeling of self-determination that accompanies our sense of controlling power . . . the abstractive character of unilateral power . . . breeds an insensitivity to the presence of the other.[14]

Loomer also contends that this conception of power has controlled the Western historical experience. Political, military, social, economic, ethical, and theological systems all presuppose strength as unilateral power. "It is rigorously operative in certain embodiments of leadership as well as in the relations between the sexes."[15] Even the Christian doctrine of love, which at first glance appears to counteract the presuppositions of unilateral power, reinforces rather than challenge its presuppositions. Love as *agape,* as self-sacrifice, is merely a reversal of the hierarchies of power and their directions of concern. Instead of power as total self-interest, the direction is reversed, shifting the balance of power, not the understanding of it. ". . . love is as unilateral and nonrelational in its way as unilateral power is in its way."[16]

With the domination of Western culture by male control and by the active suppression of those who represent nonpatriarchal views of the self and power, we have a global system of patriarchal power. Those persons, groups, or nations with less power—the poor, weak, and less developed—are accorded prestige and help in relation to their ability to wield power through their allegiances with oppressors or with superpowers. Hence, women are accorded respect or power in terms of male ownership and poorer nations have worth as potential allies to superpowers.

The Power that Nurtures Life

At this point in human history feminism presents an important alternative to death-delivering patriarchal systems. Because women have had to know and function within both male and female identity spheres in society, the feminist integration of the two is not a simple synthesis of them. The feminist integration emerges from an awareness of oppression and from a view of reality to which male identity has actively closed itself. Hence, the feminist view of self and power does not merely present an alternative, it actively calls into question the patriarchal views of self and power as illusory and destructive.

The feminist poets Susan Griffin, in *Pornography and Silence,* and Audre Lorde, in *Uses of the Erotic: The Erotic as Power,* define an integrated view of power that involves both a strong self-affirming identity and a deep connection to others. They name the power Eros.

Eros is the basic yearning for relationship. It leads us toward self-discovery and intimacy, and it affirms openness, flexibility, and the ability to change. The life-force behind the creative, empowering energy of our lives is the erotic. "The erotic is the nurturer or nursemaid of all our deepest knowledge."[17] The erotic bridges the spiritual, political, personal, and social parts of our lives by a sensual span of physical-emotional-psychic-mental elements. This span bonds "what is deepest and strongest and richest within each of us being shared: the passions of love in its deepest meanings."[18] Erotic power connects us to our bodies, our bodies to all levels of our experience, and us to others, so that differences become less threatening. Erotic power lures us toward creativity and a depth of experience that refuses to settle for mediocrity. And, finally, erotic power makes us hungry for justice in the deepest sense of being responsible to ourselves as we reject all that makes us numb to others, suffering, and self-hate. Acts against oppression become essential to ourselves, "motivated and empowered from within."[19] As the erotic functions in her life, Lorde feels led to an affirmation of herself that requires her full presence—feeling, thinking, intuiting, sensing—to herself and to others.

The power of this vision of the erotic is its inclusivity. No aspect of embodied human existence is to be repressed for the sake of control. Rather, each capacity—thinking, willing, feeling—is tied to a deep, inclusive sensuality that is grounded in connectedness. The power of the erotic is the acceptance and union of each capacity of the self with other selves.

Feminists such as Griffin and Lorde present healing alternatives to the death-delivering power systems of patriarchy. The self and power are conceived of as fundamentally relational. Hence, any worldview that identifies separation, autonomy, or alienation as the keys to self-worth and power is seen as basing itself in an inadequate understanding of reality. The feminist claim is that connectedness is the more inclusive and adequate category.

Feminist research on female identity formation confirms an orientation to self and power that is deeply relational. According to Chodorow's study, women develop a sense of identity oriented toward affiliation and affective relationships. Because women are nurtured as infants by the same-sex parent, we form personal relationships with the objects of our identification such that the female identity-forming process is more continuously embedded in and mediated by an ongoing relationship with the mother.

> Externally, as internally, women grow up and remain more connected to others. Not only are the roles which girls learn more interpersonal, particularistic, and effective than those which boys learn. Processes of identification and role learning for girls also tend to be particularistic

and affective—embedded in an interpersonal relationship with their mothers . . . Women's roles are basically familiar, and concerned with personal, affective ties . . . which require connection to, rather than separateness from, others.[20]

In addition to the general tendency toward a particularistic, affective, interpersonal orientation, Chodorow contends women feel our identity is incomplete without a complex of relationships of differing kinds. Hence most women provide a differing orientation to reality than most men, an orientation grounded in connectedness.

According to Gilligan, the female tendency to orient a sense of self around connection and complex relationships results in a different understanding of power. Power is equated with giving and with care so that acts of nurturance are understood as acts of strength. The mature feminine view of power sees the strengths of interdependence, of building up resources to give them to others, of yielding to win, and of relinquishing to gain. Involvement with others is seen as an aspect of the self's realization.

In their portrayal of relationships, women replace the bias of men toward separation with a representation of the interdependence of self and other, both in love and in work . . . women depict ongoing attachment as the path that leads to maturity. . . . Since the reality of connection is experienced by women as given rather than as freely contracted, they arrive at an understanding of life that reflects the limits of autonomy and control. As a result, women's development delineates the path not only to a less violent life but also to a maturity realized through interdependence and taking care.[21]

The basis for ethical decision making in this latter view does not lie with a balance of power. Rather, it lies with the full development and use of erotic power. The fullest capacity to maintain relationships and to hurt or harm as little as possible becomes the basis of justice. The emphasis is on preventing anyone from being hurt, and the attitude of care extends especially toward those who are least able to protect or defend themselves. Hence the shift is away from equity and reciprocity and toward generosity and care.

Chodorow and Gilligan understand the drawbacks of an extreme male view of self and power as a self-identity that is brittle and isolated, is afraid of relatedness, associating intimacy with violence, and is oriented toward the domination and control of others.

Denial of sense of connectedness and isolation of affect may be more characteristic of masculine development and may produce a rigid and punitive superego . . . (and) implacability and overrigidity. . . . Men's endopsychic object-world tends to be more fixed and . . . relational issues tend to be more repressed. . . . Masculine personality, then, comes to be defined more in terms of denial of relations . . . (and denial of femininity) . . .[22]

Conversely, Chodorow and Gilligan view the drawbacks of an extremely female self-identity as an elusive sense of self that turns to others, such as children, who are unable to fill the consuming relational needs of an insecure self; as formed by the demands relationality makes upon an internal need to nurture; and as perceiving itself as passive victim. "Feminine development . . . may lead to a superego more open to persuasion and the judgments of others . . . or instant dependence on the superego structures of another. . . . Feminine personality comes to be based less on repression or inner objects . . . and more on retention and continuity of external relationships."[23]

Both Chodorow and Gilligan believe the difficulties of these extreme masculine and feminine views of self and power are created by a society that differentiates roles hierarchically by gender and leaves the role of primary nurturer of infants to women, establishing an identity-forming system that reproduces the misogyny and sexism that create it. Each author recommends a feminist view of self and power that includes the most positive aspects of both a confident, responsible self and a deep openness to intimacy and relationality. Such a self is made extremely difficult by a society characterized by male dominance that actively seeks to prohibit the female perspective.[24]

McClelland, in his research on power, noticed that women, when they entered the competitive structures of male-dominated professions, shifted their perception of power in a traditionally masculine direction. When women are isolated from each other and are expected to perform well on male terms, we are capable of doing so. Hence, the feminist analysis of patriarchal systems, combined with a conscious awareness of the need for different modes of living and perceptions of power, must be an essential component of the movement of large numbers of women into decision-making policy positions, else women lose their grounding in erotic power and reproduce patriarchal power.[25] McClelland's observation about the shift in power orientation also provides a hope that an orientation toward unilateral power can also change.

Loomer believes relational power is the alternative to unilateral power. Relational power is the power to make and sustain mutually internal relationships. He asserts that the depth to which we are open and remain committed to relationships is the extent of our power. In this view of power the tendency to exclude others from our world of meaning and concern is an act of powerlessness and fear. To attempt to control others is to narrow our own world and its possibilities. To exist within permanently hierarchical relationships is to limit the extent to which we can receive and give in relationships. For the final source of any power is through mutually internal relationships. "'Relation' in the internal sense is a way of speaking of the presence of others in our own being. It is the peculiar destiny of process/relational modes of thought to have transformed this commonplace but deep-seated observation into a metaphysical first principle."[26]

The strength of Loomer's insight is its inclusivity, for what becomes clear from his analysis is that even unilateral power draws its life from relationships rather than from an isolated self. The difference is in how those relationships are perceived and the consequences of such perceptions in regard to self-identity. In Loomer's view unilateral power creates individuals who lack strength and stature because they are physically small and brittle. Unilateral power does not acknowledge its essential dependence on those it controls and labels as weak while depending on the "weak" for survival. Hence, the capacity for relationships within unilateral power is weak because of its self-deception. "If power always means the exercising of influence and control, and if receiving always means weakness and a lack of power, then a creative and strong love that comprises a mutual giving and receiving is not possible."[27]

Patriarchal Theology

Christian theology reflects male control and the patriarchal perspective. God is consistently, overtly imaged as male, and he possesses the highest forms of patriarchal power. Even where the claim is made that God is relational, or loving, the final reliance is upon unilateral power. Few theologies do not presuppose unilateral power. For example, we find evidence of unilateral power in many doctrines of freedom. God allows freedom to exist, but God's unilateral power can override freedom. Other examples include theological doctrines such as aseity or omnipotence.[28] In the end, most theologies rest their faith in the belief that God will triumph with a preconceived good, a good often conceived in highly patriarchal terms. Humankind does not contribute to this good except to actualize it. Only with an external, higher power in final control is a basis given for hope and faith. In many theologies, faith is pinned upon hope in an abstract future hidden from and awaited by humanity, but promised by God. The goal of faith is to receive this external good passively while working actively for its realization. Our relationship to the Word and to God is unilateral. Masculine notions of self and power are projected upon God as theological doctrines that contradict erotic power and a loving God.

The notions of erotic power as divine power and a fluid self such that self-worth is measured by one's ability to sustain mutually internal, multivalent relationships and by one's ability to exhibit care for others are not entirely missing from the Christian tradition. In the everyday lives of most people who nurture children, love friends, and heal others, erotic power is felt. Yet, a fundamental confusion exists in the lives of those who, while nurturing persons within the framework of their interpersonal relationships, affirm the maintenance of hierarchy within those relationships, worship a god of unilateral power, and support the patriarchal powers that govern the larger spheres of politics, institutions, and church structures.

It is no accident Christian theology has been reluctant to give ground in the use of a male image system. Theology has tied itself to patriarchal power and a masculine view of reality. Although other, less patriarchal views have survived within Christianity, theological systems and ecclesiastical institutions with hierarchical understandings of power have been the most reluctant to disconnect themselves from their identification with patriarchal power and its built-in misogyny.

As long as Christian theology continues to presuppose that male identity and unilateral power are descriptive of all reality, or of the highest reality, there will be a basic incoherence in the Christian concern with peace and justice. Peace and justice cannot be belated, tacked on concerns that appear after we have worked out theological systems based on unilateral power.

Christian theology and the church, although concerned about peace and justice, fail to understand that they too carry the patriarchal paradigms of the culture. They perpetuate the problem while trying to stop it. The struggle to stop nuclear weapons development and to achieve a decent life for all people is often couched in the terms of the conflict of unilateral powers, as is the theology behind such commitments.

Although a current balance of unilateral powers may succeed for a time in staying global destruction, the removal of the very real threat of such destruction cannot be conceived until the paradigms of patriarchal power are transformed. Until the bullying threats and expensive weapons of unilateral powers are understood as insane and out of touch with the reality of erotic power, we will continue to struggle for a balance of powers. If our theology continues, however subtly, to carry the same competitive message, we will be locked in the same struggle. If the views of God, self, and power that feed that struggle are not transformed, all creation may be lost forever. The paradox in this quest for transformation is that unilateral, patriarchal power is grounded in invulnerability and fear. To undergo effects, to change and be transformed, is antithetical to the maintenance of patriarchal power. What we must work toward are paradigms that do not presuppose change as the shattering of the self, but understand transformation as the creating of a greater self. As long as our social systems continue to reproduce a patriarchal male identity and attitudes of male dominance and as long as Christian theology and church structures seek, by active resistance or passive ignorance, to silence and exclude women and other oppressed peoples, the shadow of the death of creation lengthens.

A Theology of Erotic Power

Any theology grounded in erotic power makes interdependence, peace, and justice central aspects of the world's relationships. The world exists as evidence of a loving divine spirit, and that spirit is present to us in our connectedness to and our concern and care for ourselves and others. Divine reality does not consist of a will outwardly imposed upon the world from a transcendent deity, but in our awareness of the very nature of erotic power as that which emerges from within our deepest connection to ourselves, from our experience of the world as deeply internal to ourselves, and from our experience of God in the life-giving, creative power of interdependence. God as loving is present to us through our relationships to self and others. Divine will is not found in the imposition of external, abstract goals and principles upon a reluctant humanity.

Humanity is not to be valued as the hierarchical crown of creation imposing, like the patriarchal deity, its will upon the world. Rather, the entire cosmos is internally connected to our continued existence, and we have the capacity to understand the depth and breadth of that connectedness. Hence, human beings are unique in their capacity to sustain complex relationships of caring concern and mutuality via all aspects of their lives—thought, emotion, perception, volition, and sensuality. In the actualization of divine power we carry the image of the divine spirit. When we allow harm to ourselves or others, when we act out of fear and attempt to control or reject others, and when we deceive ourselves with the lie of self-sufficiency, we violate that divine spirit.

Faith in God is our ability to trust erotic power, which requires far more strength and courage than a retreat into a disconnected, private experience of a wholly transcendent deity. The leap of faith is not upward, but inward and outward at the same time. The internal strength that comes from a deep sense of personal faith does not come from the ability to be disconnected from the world, but from being connected to the world.

The personal strength that comes from faith allows us to transcend our given context because we have the capacity to carry other contexts within us. Our breadth of experience and our depth of connectedness to a wide-ranging and diverse world are what give us the gift of transcendence. Transcendence comes not from other-worldliness and disconnection but from greater connectedness, from our increasing ability to trust our relationship to a wider and wider web of reality. It is through this transcendence, a transcendence of greater relationality, that we are a creative, transforming presence in the world, for only then is God fully present to the world.

The paradox and ambivalence of transcendence is that our attachment to ideas or memories may become ways we prevent ourselves from being fully present in a given context, especially when a context threatens us. Then our capacity for relational breadth becomes a way we disconnect ourselves from others, using our transcendence to hold to objective and abstract realities that interfere with our ability to feel fully what is concretely with us. The more disconnected we become, the more we hunger for, and yet are afraid of, the experience of concrete reality. Hence, we create disciplines, such as meditation or mysticism, which require fully present, focused attention to the present moment; or we recall nostalgically moments in which we were compelled by context to be fully, deeply present, for example, the remembering of birthing stories by women or sports and combat stories by men.

The religious dimension in these experiences of full presence is in the union of the self's focused presence and heightened awareness of reality with a deep awareness of transcendence through the connection to a larger purpose or world that lies beyond the individual. When transcendence is experienced through full presence in reality, we experience a heightened awareness, a special aliveness, and an excellence that transforms our existence. The tragedy of patriarchal culture is its attempt to confine and control such experiences of transcendence by limiting the kind of relationships persons can have to gender-linked tasks and roles. Such control tends to kill the experiences themselves.

A further ambiguity of transcendence that comes from the depth and breadth of connectedness is the chaos that dances at the edge of our awareness. To be fully open to relationality always carries the threat that, in internalizing reality, the self will not be able to make life cohere and will dissolve into identification with its world without a sense of its own participation as a self in that reality. Dissolution and loss of self are the risks required in creating erotic power, and chaos is the matrix from which creativity and a distinct sense of self emerge. Hence an acceptance of, rather than denial of, chaos as the factor in our lives that allows for relationality and change, which are essential to the ability to sustain mutually internal relationships.

Chaos does not kill, it creates. Control kills. Hence, evil emerges from fear and the need to control with unilateral power. Unilateral power attempts to control and confine others so the self as invulnerable is not threatened. Unilateral power divides the world into friends and enemies and seeks to destroy the enemy. Unilateral power controls aspects of self and others in an attempt to dominate the world for its use. Unilateral power carries the curses of injustice and war and lies at the root of evil.

In "Only Justice Can Stop a Curse," Alice Walker examines an old curse of revenge that American blacks wished upon their white oppressors.[29] The curse seems now close to fulfillment, especially with the threat of nuclear devastation. But Walker asserts that revenge on an enemy, especially when revenge is self-destructive, is not real satisfaction, if for no other reason than that life is better than death. Walker chooses an act she feels is the only protection from the curse of nuclear death. "I intend to protect my home. Praying—not a curse—only that my courage will not fail my love. But if by some miracle, and all our struggle, the earth is spared, only justice to every living thing (and everything is alive) will save humankind. And we are not saved yet."[30]

Walker rejects revenge and accepts the task of realizing erotic power. The courage to love and to speak of divine power as the life-giving gift of loving means to understand the divine-human relationship as one of interdependence. God is our lover, as we are lovers of each other and of every living thing. Our ability to recognize our interdependence will save us. The ways we cocreate ourselves, each other, and God will bring us to a full realization of peace and justice.

Peace and justice lie at the heart of a truly relational view of the world, and they lie at the heart of a deep love for all creation. In her novel *The Color Purple,* Walker presents a vision of God that heals and empowers persons, even in the most destitute situations. Her vision is tough-minded but compassionate, simple yet rich.

> God love everything you love—and a mess of stuff you don't. But more than anything else, God love admiration . . . God . . . just wanting to share a good thing. I think it pisses God off if you walk by the color purple in a field somewhere and don't notice it . . . People think pleasing God is all God care about. But any fool living in the world can see (God) always trying to please us back . . . always making little surprises and springing them on us when us least expect. (God) want to be loved . . . Everything want to be loved.[31]

Walker's heroines find their vision of God and are sustained by that vision as they survive the depths of destitution and despair. They are empowered and made whole by their ability to love in the face of unilateral powers that threaten to destroy them.

Theology that leads us toward life-giving realities must ground itself in erotic power. The injustice of rich nations that dominate and shape the world at the expense of all of creation and the lingering threat of nuclear devastation can be overcome if we learn to think and see beyond unilateral power. Our theology must work to lead us toward visions of a whole, healed life in which everything is loved.

NOTES

1. This slogan of the peace movement is the title of Dorothee Soelle's book, *The Arms Race Kills Even Without War* (Philadelphia: Fortress Press, 1983).
2. The extent of the continued exploitation of the Pacific Islands is described in the August 1983 issue of *Sojourners* magazine, 12, no. 7.
3. Data found in a Think-About guide called "Wage Peace—Fight Hunger," published by a consortium of organizations. Available from Bea Rothenbuecher, 19 East 88th Street, New York, New York 10028.
4. Soelle, *The Arms Race Kills Even Without War,* 3.
5. "Wage Peace", 2.
6. Essays on the compatibility of Buddhist and process metaphysics can be found in John B. Cobb, Jr., *Beyond Dialogue: Toward a Mutual Transformation of Christianity and Buddhism* (Philadelphia: Fortress Press, 1982), 145–50; and in Jay McDaniel, "Zen and the Self," *Process Studies,* [Journal of Process Studies at School of Theology, Claremont, Calif.] 10, nos. 3–5, (1971), 110–19.
7. Conversations with Dorothy Bass, assistant professor of church history, Chicago Theological Seminary, about her dissertation on feminism and pacifism.
8. Susan Griffin, "The Way of All Ideology," *Signs,* 7, no. 3, (1982), 641–60.
9. Nancy Chodorow, *The Reproduction of Mothering: Psychoanalysis and the Sociology of Gender* (Berkeley: The University of California Press, 1978), 4.
10. Ibid., 9.
11. Ibid., 182.
12. Bernard Loomer, "Two Conceptions of Power," *Process Studies,* 6, no. 2, (1976), 5–32.
13. Ibid., 16.
14. Ibid., 17–18.
15. Ibid., 19.
16. Ibid.
17. Audrey Lorde, *Uses of the Erotic: The Erotic as Power* (Brooklyn: Out and Out Books, 1978), 4.
18. Ibid., 4.
19. Ibid., 7.
20. Chodorow, *The Reproduction of Mothering,* 177–79.
21. Carol Gilligan, *In a Different Voice: Psychological Theory and Women's Development* (Cambridge: Harvard University Press, 1982), 170, 172.
22. Chodorow, *The Reproduction of Mothering,* 169.
23. Ibid.
24. Ibid. Chodorow goes further in her study by tying the current social chaos and breakdown of the nuclear family in the United States to the structures that create it. Hence, the response of reassertion of traditional family struc-

tures and values to solve the crisis only heightens the difficulty. "Those very capacities and needs which create women as mothers create potential contradictions in mothering . . . In a society where women do meaningful productive work, have ongoing adult companionship while they are parenting, and have satisfying emotional relationships with other adults, they are less likely to overinvest in children. But these are precisely the conditions that capitalist industrial development has limited . . . Contemporary problems in mothering emerge from potential internal contradictions in family and the social organization of gender—between women's mothering and individuation in daughters, between emotional connection and a sense of masculinity in sons. Changes generated from outside the family, particularly in the economy, have sharpened these contradictions," 211–13.

25. David McClelland's research also highlights the difficulty of tokenism. When women and minorities are isolated from support groups and forced to participate on the terms of the dominant class, they take on the values of the dominant class in order to survive, *Power: The Inner Experience* (New York: Irvington Publishers, Inc., 1975).

26. Loomer, "Two Conceptions of Power," 22.

27. Ibid., 21.

28. Extensive work on the theological problem of omnipotence and aseity has been done by Charles Hartshorne, for example in *The Divine Relativity: A Social Conception of God,* (New Haven: Yale University Press, 1948) and *The Logic of Perfection,* (LaSalle, Ill.: Open Court Publishing Company, 1962).

29. Alice Walker, "Only Justice Can Stop a Curse," *Reweaving the Web of Life: Feminism and Nonviolence,* ed. Pam McAllister, (Philadelphia: New Society Publishers, 1982).

30. Ibid., 265.

31. Alice Walker, *The Color Purple,* (New York: Harcourt Brace Jovanovich, Publishers, 1982), 167–68.

3

God and the National State

DAYA KRISHNA

God as a term denoting that which is ultimately real and absolutely valuational is simultaneously the necessary presupposition of all thought and action and also their ultimate goal. Yet, it is equally true that it is neither known nor even knowable in principle, in the sense that any finite being or set of such beings may hope to know it in any determinate manner. Being generally conceived as beyond both space and time and transcending them in the sense that, even when considered as immanent in the world, it can never be regarded as completely revealed at any particular point in space or time, it cannot but be unknown and unknowable in the deepest sense of the word. Yet, however paradoxical the idea of God may be, it is a symbol of that which man as a self-conscious reflective being, who both knows and acts, has to encounter at every turn.

However, most action and thought presupposes not merely a thinker or an actor, but a collectivity of thinkers and actors, that is, a plurality of such beings without whom it is impossible to conceive of the possibility of either knowledge or of action in any significant sense of the terms. The relationship to God, on the other hand, is primarily perceived in relation to the individual as *apart from* others. In the well-known phrase of the mystics, it is the flight of the alone to the alone that defines the relationship. The relationship with God, or what may be called the turning of human consciousness toward God, is in all traditions a turning away from the world, including the withdrawal from concern for other human beings as well as the concern for one's own embodied self, that is, the life of one's own body and mind, intellect and life.

Even when traditional thinking about God has tried to make it relevant to man's concern with other beings, as in the ideal of the Bodhisattva or in that of "loving one's neighbor," it has remained only at the periphery of religious thought rather than at its center; and even when a religion has been primarily an affair of the community or group—as in Islam, Judaism, and Christianity, as well as in some devotional sects in Hinduism where it is said that God is present where devotees sing his name or where the community of faithful gathers together—others are always excluded, i.e., those who are not totally of the faith or who do not belong to the group or the church concerned.

The question, thus, has always been: what to do with those who are outside the faith or who belong to a different one. What is the relation of the God of one's community, faith, or religion to those who do not believe in him and thus are outside the sect or church to which God is exclusively confined by his followers? The proselytizing religions have usually demanded from others conversion or death, or some sort of inferior status in society if they could not be converted or eliminated. Even those religions that fundamentally believe each group or person has a right to have a God of his or her own choice normally feel that they have a positive superiority to those members of the community or society who believe in some other God or choose a form of God that is other than their own.

Yet however great the problem of reconciling the universality that any concept of God inevitably claims for itself and the equally inevitable pluralistic situation in which diverse churches and religions find themselves, there is the other deeper problem with respect to the community that at least formally believes in the same God. The relations between human beings or between groups and states belonging to the same religion do not seem to be any better than those between believers in different religions. Being a Muslim or a Christian or a Hindu does not in any significant way lead to a type of behavior toward others of the same religion that may be regarded as distinct from the behavior one displays toward persons belonging to a religion other than one's own, except in the marginal sense that one is perhaps less likely to come into intimate contact with them. The history of relations between states and kingdoms belonging to the same religion does not offer striking evidence of any difference in their behavior ascribable to the fact that they professed the same identical religion. Rather, like individuals in conflict, they invoke the same God for the preferment of their own ends.

The problem thus may be posed in a threefold manner: one concerning God and his relationship with an individual in his personal, private, and innermost life, a relationship that has only a marginal influence on one's empirical life, which primarily consists of life in society and with relationship to others. The second is concerned with the relationship between God and social groups or communities in which people live in society. The third is a relationship between God and the political units that in modern times consist of nation-states. As far as the first is concerned, even if the idea of God makes any relevant difference in one's empirical life, it does so primarily through the individual in his or her private, personal capacity alone. On the other hand, when one functions in a public capacity, which is essentially representative in character, one inevitably has to express in some particular, specific form the interests of all those who subscribe to diverse forms of religion if the society happens to be multireligious in character. This may assume the form of allowing each to pursue his or her own path, provided it does not come into conflict with others, a situation that is in principle possible only if the other also believes in the same principle. But how can the relationship between nation-states be governed by a consciousness of God, which necessarily transcends and encompasses the differences between the nation-states themselves?

In a certain sense bringing God into any discussion is, essentially, to close it; though from another point of view it is true that it also makes us aware of the parochial limitations of the discussion and helps us realize the arbitrariness of the boundaries we ourselves set. To bring the consideration of God into any consideration of the relation between nation-states or between any other groups or set of groups, whether religious or nonreligious, is to bring an awareness to all concerned that they should think about issues from the viewpoint of the other and, ultimately, from the viewpoint of that which transcends not merely themselves, but the other also.

There is, however, an aspect of the matter that we must take note of if we do not want our discussion to be superficial and blind toward an essential feature of the situation. The relation between nation-states, or even between groups, is mediated by persons who act not on their own, but in a representative capacity, that is, as responsible for persons other than themselves rather than as persons responsible for their own selves. The difference between private and public is overriding in this regard, and as Hannah Arendt has pointed out so well, the realm of the polity is the realm of the public par excellence. Of course, she emphasizes the negative aspect of the term *private,* which no religion can accept as in the religious context. The term *private* denotes the most meaningful experience that has been known to man up until now. In fact, the positive sense of the term *private* in modern times relates it primarily to what is called one's life, not for God, but in relation to other human beings with whom one has affective relationships. In fact, the hard core of what is regarded as private is basically what one concerns oneself with and wherein one is primarily responsible to oneself. The reference to others is not only minimal, but basically instrumental. Ultimately, one is concerned with oneself alone.

The private thus does not belong to the realm of morals, where one is primarily concerned with others and not with what happens to oneself. But even the realm of morals is primarily concerned with the relationship between individuals or persons. The relations between groups or between an individual and a group are not exactly defined in terms of moral values, but rather in terms of rules, which tend to define the structure of essentially undefined and unstructured relationships in this domain. The problem of institutional morality, i.e., the problem of morality in the interactions between institutions, has not been explored to the same extent as has individual morality. The reason relationships between institutions happen to be of a negative character relates to the fact that the relationship is primarily one of competition rather than cooperation. And even when it is a relationship of cooperation, it is only in the context of interests rather than values, and that too only temporarily until it suits the parties concerned. The heart of morality, on the other hand, lies in the sacrifice of interests for the sake of values and the sacrifice of one's interests for the sake of the interests of others or for the value or values they pursue.

These sacrifices, which are involved in the very nature of value, may be accepted in the context of interaction between persons, but can never be given even a marginal place in the relationship between organizations. In the case of institutions, to sacrifice one's interests would be almost tantamount to what has come to be called "treason" in the political domain. Yet, if considerations of God—that is, considerations pertaining to value and reality that transcend one's own group—are to be brought to bear on the thinking about relations between nation-states, then a fundamental change will have to occur in the way we perceive these relations, the terms in which we describe them, and the criteria by which we judge or evaluate them. The task of formulating these terms and these criteria seems to be the central one that all persons who seriously entertain the idea of God must undertake nowadays.

The relations between nation-states, or even between different polities in the past that did not perceive themselves as nations in the modern sense, have always been governed by the idea of potential hostility between them. Basically, the terms in which this relationship has been perceived are *victor* and *vanquished, conqueror* and *conquered.* Even in cases where, as in certain traditions in ancient India, the relationship has been perceived in terms of suzerainty rather than sovereignty, the ideal for any polity has always been imperialist expansion, the conquering of other territories, the idea of a *Chakravartin,* i.e., of a ruler whose sway is acknowledged by all, even if de facto control is left to the previous rulers of the centuries on the regions concerned. It was always considered the duty of a king to expand his frontiers and the domain of his rule as far as possible. The neighboring kingdoms, therefore, were always to be treated not as allies or friends, but rather as enemies, a theory fully formulated in Kautilya's *Arthashastra,* the ancient Indian treatise on the science and art of politics.

It is perhaps to the credit of modern times that this doctrine, which seemed so self-evident to political thinkers in the past, has not only been questioned, but regarded as unacceptable. A change in rhetoric, however, does not necessarily mean that the realities have also changed. The notion of spheres of influence, elaborated in recent times and the emergence of the notion of client states whose support and vote one may always count upon, is an eloquent reminder of the fact that the ghost of the past has not been completely exorcised from the political practice of nations even today. Yet, it is equally true that the rights of autonomy, independence, and noninterference are claimed and acknowledged at least on the verbal level by most nations today, and that the very notion of non-colonialism underlines the fact that control of other states or even the influencing of their policies is to be achieved these days by means different from those that were not only prevalent in the past, but also accepted as correct. Large scale aid, both military and economic, is proof that nation-states today are supposed to have obligations to other nation-states, which they are expected to fulfill; if they do not, they are subjected to censure. It is true that all the attempts for building a new international economic order have failed to make any headway, despite repeated meetings on the subject. It is also true that most nations have not felt it either desirable or feasible to fulfill their obligations in this regard. Still, all nations today do give some money to international organizations, which in their turn do perform certain international functions, including giving aid to those who need it. There are also major bilateral agreements that are expected to achieve the same purpose, though perhaps with more direct political implications. It is imperative, therefore, that certain criteria and norms be laid down for the conditions and forms that bilateral, multilateral, or international aid may take in modern times.

The relations between nation-states have to be thought of in more positive terms, and the first precondition of this is that they should be conceived of in relation to the welfare of the other state rather than one's own state. Of course, there would always be the perennial problem of how to distinguish between the good of the people and the good of the rulers of the state. The problem arises with respect to one's own state also, as one who rules tends to identify one's own interests with that of the people over whom one rules. The problem is difficult to resolve. It may be true that, even when one's actions toward another state are not guided primarily by reference to the good of one's own state, it is difficult to decide how to perceive the good of the other state. In many cases, especially where the other state is ruled by a tyrant, it may be difficult not to act in such a manner that one's actions may be seen as counter to the interests of that state.

To take a concrete example, how would one regard India's military intervention in support of the revolt in East Pakistan against the Pakistan authorities, an intervention that led to the creation of the free state of Bangladesh out of the dismemberment of the former state of Pakistan, which comprised both West and East Pakistan. If one thinks only in terms of nation-states as formal entities, then it is obvious that the Indian intervention cannot be regarded as governed by the good of the nation-state of Pakistan. But if the interests of the nation-state are seen in terms of the interests of the people, then a different conclusion would have to be drawn. The logic of the argument, however, can always be stretched to the extreme, where all interventions, whether military or nonmilitary, may be formally justified in the name of the interests of the people, as has been done by the revolutionary subversion in the so-called interests of the people by communist regimes all over the world. In fact, the safeguarding of democracy has led perhaps to as many interventions in recent history as the safeguarding of socialism.

Still, it may be assumed that any type of aid that makes a country self-reliant can be regarded as motivated by the desire to do good for that country. It is, of course, true that even this minimal concept raises problems both at the theoretical and applied levels. At the theoretical level, the concept of self-reliance leads ultimately to the notion of monads, which are completely windowless and thus closed to all influences from the outside, leading to a world where there is no interaction between different entities—a situation which can hardly be considered desirable from either the moral or the social point of view. In applied fields, it leads to the notion of autarchy and a denial of the possibility of enrichment by interchange with others. In fact, the concept of dependence itself seems to require a thorough analysis in the context of relations both between individuals and between groups and nation-states.

But, however difficult it may be to understand these concepts in an unambiguous manner, it is fairly clear that there is a type of interchange in the relationship both between persons and groups that are asymmetrically situated in terms of knowledge or power or wealth that decreases the asymmetry to some extent and, at a deeper level, fosters capacities that lead them not only to grow on their own, but also to innovate in new directions so that each is not merely helpful to itself, but also contributes to the growth and development of the erstwhile superior party in the relationship. Perhaps the concepts of self-reliance and interdependence have to be supplemented by concepts of enrichment and innovation. The relationship between nation-states has been seen too much in terms of the asymmetries of power or wealth and not in such a multifaceted manner that no country is regarded as superior to another in all respects, and that each is superior to the other only in some aspects and each always has something to give and take in a process of mutual enrichment leading to the growth of mankind as a whole.

It is well known that a teacher learns from students almost as much as students learn from a teacher, even though the process of learning in the two cases is very different. But it is not so well recognized that groups and nations are in the same situation, even if not to the same degree. A self-conscious awareness of this dimension of interchange between cultures and nations may perhaps lead to a different view of the relations between them than the notions prevalent at present help to foster.

The infusion of the awareness of God in the relationship between nation-states, or even the raising of the issue or bringing the two concepts together into a common focus, is basically to challenge human awareness into making an attempt to transcend its narrow, parochial concerns, as well as to think not only in terms of humanity as a whole, but also to widen one's awareness in the attempt to comprehend the totality and feel responsible for it. The concepts of "collective responsibility" and "responsibility toward a collectivity" have to be explored in greater depth than has been done up until now in human thought.

The awareness of God, or rather of that which is symbolized by the term, normally takes man away from a concern with temporal reality, particularly that which is sociopolitical in nature and is involved in history and time. Some recent thinkers, such as Sri Aurobindo and Teilhard de Chardin, have tried to remedy this defect in traditional thought that has concerned itself seriously with the religious dissension of human experience. But even they have not dealt with the problems raised by nation-states and the interrelationship between them or by the fact that an individual is not a world citizen but only of one particular country or another.

The recent issues in the theory of choice and welfare have primarily been conceived of in terms of the policies of nation-states with respect to the welfare of their own citizens. How these policies should affect the welfare of the citizens of other countries is usually ignored in the debate. There is much thought regarding the adoption of policies that lead to the betterment of the least advantaged member or group in society. But there is very little talk of adopting policies that are to the advantage of the least advantaged nations in the world. How far the thinking has gone in the social sciences is still determined by the realities of the nation-state, and one's subconscious identification with it is seen by the conspicuous absence of any sustained discussion regarding the achievement of welfare not within nation-states but between nation-states.

The popularity of the rhetoric of freedom and welfare shows the immense influence of liberal and socialist thought in the political domain. But there is no comparable rhetoric that could be said to pervade the talk about the relations between nations. There is, of course, the talk of noninterference in each other's affairs and agreements of trade and cultural exchanges, but there is little else. It only shows that international relations are conceived of more in terms of problems of power generated by facts of geopolitical situations of countries, as well as the world power structure obtaining at a particular time. Of course, most of the time rhetoric is *only* rhetoric, but one should not forget that it is also evidence that these are the values accepted by the consciousness of both the elite and the illiterate masses at large and that, however half-heartedly, there is an attempt by the governing states to justify themselves by the actions they undertake toward the realization of those values. Similarly, if the considerations urged above are brought to bear on our thinking about the relations between nation-states, the result may be the adoption of a new rhetoric, which would at least give some indication of what *ought* to obtain in these relationships.

It may be asked: why should we bring in the notion of God to do this job? Will it not be better if we use some other word to convey the same idea? After all, many people are allergic to the word itself, and most people tend to interpret it in the way they have been brought to understand it through the respective religions in which they happened to have been raised. There is substance to this criticism, but for any person genuinely interested in religion, the notion of God refers to something that transcends the particular religion to which he or she belongs. Anyone who is concerned with the world in however small a measure and feels some obligation toward it should try to bring the two concerns together, one of which is primarily concerned with the transcendent and the other with the world.

Yet, as everybody knows, what ultimately matters is not the world, but what it *means* to us and what we *do* to it. The concern of this chapter has been to bring into one focus these two ultimate concerns of man. The former is symbolized by that which is denoted in most traditions by the term *God* or its equivalent, and the latter by such terms as *society* and *state*. The two, society and state, are not the same, but they have tended to be used in the same way in recent times, and the state has been given greater importance than society in an era when planning, development, and welfare have become the central concerns of the polity. So it is the latter that has begun to preponderate in the context of action, and hence God and the nation-states are the two poles of man's seeking at present. It has been the purpose of this chapter to bring the two into active interrelationship with each other and suggest the possibility of a meaningful interaction between the two.

4

Divine Discontent: Religious Vision and Human Transformation

KATHLEEN DUGAN

A somewhat surprising sight greets the eyes of modern religion watchers—one that is guaranteed to disturb the individual conscience and trouble the memory of the history of religion's presence in human civilizations. With unprecedented vigor, religion seems to have abandoned its proper concerns (symbolized for a wide number of people by the goal of transcendence and its lofty environs) and taken up work that broaches upon social and political concerns. This is not only a strange and alarming sight to Americans, but one that raises questions in other places where the shocks of a brutal century have deepened the privatization of religion. However, this immersion in the social order seems a crucial element of late-twentieth-century religion, and one that manifests a qualitative movement ahead in its evolutionary process, rather than, as its critics would suggest, a loss of authentic self-consciousness. The phenomenon raises questions that touch both the protagonists of religion's involvement and the social situation order that has elicited such a response.

This chapter will reflect on the relationship of religion to the crisis posed by the troubled relationships of rich and poor nations, and it will do so from the perspective of contemporary Catholic theology (with implicit recognition of the urgency of this issue in the whole of the Christian tradition, as well as in the world's religions.) To do so, a preliminary inquiry will be made into the images of God arising out of scriptural consideration of social justice and move from there to the shape of divine discontent as it dynamically affects the followers of religion. The core of the chapter, however, will focus on a specific problem that the Christian religion acknowledges as an urgent issue at all times and in all ages—i.e., how a religion can convey its essential vision so that it becomes the motive for a praxis that is understood as necessary to religion's goal: human transformation. In this specific case, it is the teaching of social justice that focuses concern on how it can assume in each generation of Christians a primary place in religious development. Within the developmental model of religious faith, there remains the pressing need to recognize the problem of nurturing continual personal transformation (or conversion, as the ancient Christian writers called it). This chapter seeks to explore the structure of that ongoing process through the lens of contemporary theological and psychological models of faith. Within the context of the current views of the religious self as member of an ecumenical, world-connected community, the ideal of religious transformation will be seen as not only profoundly personal, but as necessarily social. Thus the narrow path to fullness of life will be seen to lead not away from the world, but into the heart of its action. This is not new, but we live in an age in which it must be newly affirmed if religion is to remain true to its vision of God and responsive to the human condition. Now, as in times past, such a concept serves as a strong critique of the solipsism and apathy that are the recurring concerns of a healthy human society.

The crisis of contemporary social reality is both statistically obvious and easily apparent to the eye of an ordinary observer. Rapid flow of information makes us inescapably aware of the dilemma of most of the world and unremittingly accuses the rich and powerful nations of complicity in this state of affairs. Among firsthand witnesses of the anguish this situation entails, few are more respected than Dom Helder Camara, shepherd of the church in the northeast of Brazil. Speaking to the World Council of Churches in 1970, he posed the delegates a troubling question. In brief, he stated figures that conveyed with great clarity the enormity of the imbalance between the rich and poor nations and indicated the scant hope that this situation will change without drastic measures. The small segment of humanity that is rich prospers, while the rest (the majority) struggle in varying degrees of poverty and know their prison to be solid. The irony of this situation should not escape us; for the first time in history, we are in a position to fulfill the command of the creator to dominate nature and to complete his work of creation. We now have the technology to enable us to promote the good of every person and of the whole race. Yet the likelihood is that we will not. Camara reflects upon this in biblical terms by describing the cause of resistance to overcoming this evil in terms of blindness. And then he sums up his argument by saying that the real problem is the *First* World (the privileged part of humanity), which bears a special responsibility by reason of its prosperity, and an even greater blame because these nations are, by and large, Christian, and possess both the criteria for recognizing the sin and a prophetic tradition that urges them to be active agents in reducing the evils in history.[1]

This anomaly has not been missed by the churches. The recent convocation of the World Council of Churches spent considerable time discussing the problems inherent in the relationship of peace and social justice, and the recent papal and episcopal statements from the Roman Catholic church continually restate the necessity of the work of justice if there is to be peace at all. In a key statement, the 1971 synod of bishops introduced its reflections on the meaning of justice in the world society in this way: "Actions on behalf of justice and participation in the transformation of the world fully appear to us as a constitutive dimension of the preaching of the gospel, or, in other words, of the Church's mission for the redemption of the human race and its liberation from every oppressive situation" (*Justice in the World,* p. 34).[2] It is necessary to note that this was *not* an uncontroversial statement, and that may help to explain why it has so slowly found its way into Christian consciousness. The vision is there, and it is clear, but it has not been heard in the manner and to the degree that it must be. It is logical that this should be a matter of grave concern to the Christian churches. The problem would seem to be twofold: that of formulation in the theological tradition and transmission in the area of pastoral ministry.

The theological tradition has responded with incisive images and an instinctual awareness that the passion of religion for issues of social justice is inherent to its nature. The roots of such concepts lie deep in the Judeo-Christian tradition and should be briefly noted, since they indicate the genesis of religious concern in this area. The foundations of the biblical image of God are laid down in the book of Genesis. There, in the account of the Creation and the Fall, God is portrayed as involved in his creation. Not simply content to rest in aesthetic contemplation of his handiwork, he makes his presence known to his intelligent creatures. In the midst of their errant behavior, Genesis shows God searching for his loved ones. "Adam, where are you?" This theme, once begun, reasserts itself continually throughout the entire scriptural narrative. Perhaps the epitome of its statement occurs in Luke 15:11–32, in the parable of the prodigal son.[3] This love for his creation is depicted as passionate and concerned. Frequently it finds voice to mourn the catastrophic destruction that human beings bring on themselves. Thus, an oracle of the valley of vision in Isaiah 22 expresses God's love and consequent anguish over the carnage: "Turn your eyes away from me; leave me to weep in misery. Do not thrust consolation on me for the ruin of my people" (Isa. 22:4).[4]

This love alternately speaks in tones of pained love and of anger that seeks to restore the relationship between God and humanity. The Asian theologian Choan-Seng Song has brilliantly illumined this characteristic of God's love by relating it to the pregnant Chinese phrase *Thun-ai,* which translates as "pain-love." This paradoxical phrase evokes the passionate nature of love, which reacts in profoundly involved responses to the situation of the loved one. In certain instances, this love manifests itself in puzzlement, anguish, and consternation. It is love reaching out to those who do not reciprocate it, and it contains a restless desire to pursue and win that love. The Hebrew equivalent of this word is *hesed;* the Greek is *agape.* Song suggests that the pain-love of God is powerfully presented in John 3:16, where the logic of that love is shown to be extreme self-sacrifice.[5] In line with the entire Christian tradition, Song interprets this passage as revealing Jesus as the supreme gift of the Father's love.

Another dimension of the scriptural message reflects what God desires as fitting response from his creation. In the prophetic tradition this emerges most strikingly in a negative fashion. The consistent concern of God for the poor and the oppressed receives passionate attention when the rich and powerful choose to ignore their plight. In the eighth century B.C.E., the prophet Amos spoke of divine outrage at the terrible impact of Israel's preparations for war in the lives of the poor. His judgment is that justice is terribly distorted. Amos 3:9–10 utters this indictment: "Assemble yourselves upon the mountains of Samaria, and see the great tumult within her, and see the oppression in her midst." Says the Lord: "They do not know how to do right, those who store up violence and robbery in their strongholds." Amos 5:12 elaborates this: "For I know how many are your transgressions, and how great are your sins, you who afflict the righteous, who take a bribe, and turn aside the needy the gate." The striking parallel to modern times should be noted; the money that could be used to feed the poor and correct the balance of social justice is poured into armaments instead.

Indeed, the centrality of justice in the Bible emerges in a careful critique of its teaching. In a recent article, the moral theologian Dan Maguire draws together the evidence and suggests that justice and love are really hyphenated in the Bible, in a way that brings "good news to the poor" (Luke 4:18). Then he makes the point that there is a unified picture of God's justice throughout Scripture. It emerges as a central characteristic of God, who is portrayed as a lover of justice (Ps. 99:4) who finds his delight in it (Jer. 9:23). His holiness is manifested in terms of God's justice (Isa. 5:16). And it is this justice that we are asked to reflect in authenticating our love of him. So vital is justice that it is truly the sacrament of encounter with God, for in doing justice we incarnate in our small way God's justice and thus become holy with this holiness.[6]

It is for that reason that Deuteronomy 15:5 emphatically legislates that there shall be no poor in Israel, for their presence is a vivid indication of the people's failure to know and practice God's love. Finally, Maguire stresses that the justice of which the Bible speaks is *preemptive,* for it deals with God's positive actions in creating and preserving community, with special care given to its marginal members.[7]

There is a correlate to the concept of God in the quest for the roots of concern for social justice. Theology acknowledges as a central component of any belief system the concepts exploring the nature of humanity. The concept of justice only attains its full significance against the background of this understanding. The human person emerges in this light as a relational being, first and most obviously as defined by the status he or she holds before God. But the relation is not purely vertical; its other pole is the sense of human solidarity that is part of the Hebrew worldview from Genesis through Revelation. Israel's understanding of the people of God knows itself as sharing in a communal unity that is founded on the definitive boundaries of human existence—creation and God's eschatological reign. A shared origin and destiny contribute to the awareness of the commonality of life lived before God, in which the community as a whole is heir to the gifts of God's creation. Denial of these gifts is naturally interpreted in terms of a fracturing of the covenant that binds person to person and the community to God. Injustice becomes the sign of the failure of the love owed to God. The Christian Scriptures contain a new concept crafted by Paul to express the lived experience of the redemption brought by Christ. In the image of the Body of Christ he condenses the revelation that we are all members of the one body that is Christ, for we were created in his image, and our redemption has been gained by him. Of this enormous gift, we are the beneficiaries. Moreover, we receive with it the commission to do the works of God. In this body we belong to one another, as well as to God, and this knowledge should commit us to the welfare of the entire community. But it is in Matthew that the strongest and clearest teaching is given. The startling revelation of Matthew 25 offers an image of the final judgment where all will be judged—not on power or achievement—but on the works of charity embodied in compassion. Only those who do so earn the recognition of God.

The concepts of a belief system are worth nothing if they do not find incarnation in the living out of that tradition by its members. Thus we are led to the spirituality that informs a community, and we must ask whether Christian spirituality holds within it the power to embrace the prophetic tradition and the gospel images of the passionate God who came to dwell among us and thus form its members as active participants in the salvation of the entire human community.

One convinced spokesman for the affirmative is Matthew Lamb, who, in several recent works (most notably in his book *Solidarity with Victims*), has dealt with this issue extensively. Lamb points to the dimension of Christian spirituality that has enthusiastically embraced social justice as the most necessary work of this period of history. Indeed, he argues that this kind of spirituality is so essential that without it the following of Christ is not complete. It is not, therefore, the call of *some* Christians to immerse themselves in the work of justice and do so by a transforming solidarity with the victims of this world. It is the essential duty of every Christian's spiritual journey.[8] Granting that recent centuries have yielded to the temptation of privatized religion, and so separated the dual vocations of Christians (that of union with God and the vocation to engage in social justice ministries), Lamb interprets this breakdown in terms of a wider situation in which society was becoming increasingly secularized, and religion was relegated to the sphere of the supernatural and mystical. He analyzes this as a peculiar form of bifurcated conscience, which arose in post-Enlightenment Christianity in the Western world.[9] In his view, this does terrible violence to Christian spirituality, for religion cannot survive if it does not manifest its power for good in the social arena. Alexis de Toqueville remarked, in his study of democracy in America, that religion cannot remove itself from doing the work of justice, else it betray the sacred trust it has been given for the preservation of the common good.[10]

For Lamb, Christian spirituality is specified by a call, an imperative to live out a discipleship of faith, hope, and love, and the grace of our redemption empowers us to respond through personal *and* social transformation. A crucial element of the conversion process is the regaining of a genuine God-consciousness, of which the hallmark is that the person who lives within it is impelled to seek out solidarity with the poor, the oppressed, and the victims of history in their struggles for justice and freedom. Yet how poorly practiced or understood has this genuine Christian spirituality been in modern times! The more common scene has been blind collusion with the powers of technology, industry, and government, and a more than tacit acceptance of the power elites of the new bourgeoisie. In both capitalist and communist societies, depersonalizing and dehumanizing injustices grew as the bases of power took root and grew strong. Today, however, the cries of the poor are insistently raised toward the strongholds of power and prosperity. They cannot be ignored, for as Lamb so beautifully says, if we harden our hearts and close our minds, we run the terrifying risk of shutting out the voice of the living God.[11]

There are two areas that deserve further comment. The first is that both in Scripture and in the social reality that frames the inquiry of contemporary theology, sin has received a social definition. Rather than present it as a matter between the individual and God, the stronger witness of the traditions states that sin is, from beginning to end, a social matter. This has particular meaning in our discussion of social justice, for it would seem that sin of this nature has the ugliest form of all and is the most open to divine discontent. Second, the fact that social justice emerges as the other side of the struggle for holiness implies that, if enough Christians are faithful to their call, there will be a powerful effect on the structures of society. This effect may indeed be misunderstood in revolutionary terms, but without the threat of violence. Christian spirituality is, in this reading, liberation theology, for its passion is to see the justice that is the desire of God realized in every human situation.

The issue of an authentic spirituality offers an intensive focus for exploring the questions raised by juxtaposing religion and social reality, specifically the guilt-ridden relation of rich and poor nations. It only yields its greatest insights, however, when it is moved from the level of intellectual ideal to its realization in practical living.

Clearly, one of the major problems of any religious tradition is how best to convey the vision and consequent praxis to those who require initiation in each generation. That problem never receives a final resolution, since the changing circumstances of each era mandate reformulation of the foundational experience of that period. That project is the task of theology, and the first part of this chapter has indicated in summary fashion the revolution of thought that has been developing in modern times as the issue of the relation of religion and social reality has been recast. The correlative need of a religious tradition is to discover how the formation of its members can facilitate the passing down of the principal ideals of its theological vision. In other words, how can passion for the world, which is so profound a mark of the concept of God, be conveyed to those whose initiation into the religious community is meant to be the gate through which they enter upon a way of imitation of and correspondence with divine law?

Brief reflection, with some help from history, quickly reveals that this problem is as great a concern for the Christian tradition as it is for many others, for on its resolution depends the continuing existence of a vital community of faith. Particularly in a tradition in which infant baptism has become normative, the evolution of religious awareness and an authentic consciousness poses enormous difficulties. Seasons of declension in religious vitality or unsettling environmental conditions elicit new attempts to advance the success of educating the members of a religious tradition in primary values. The insights of modern psychology have contributed eminently to the models of religious growth that are being proposed today. Each of the models offers a perspective in which religious development is seen as part of the total evolution of the person, and thus the conversion that is required for full religious evolution is a complex phenomenon. Examples both old and new abound; let us study several as they speak from different angles on the process of religious conversion.

The choice of the word *conversion* in this discussion arose from several considerations. Examination of the essential content of the goal of perfection that has been so extensively interpreted in the history of the Christian tradition suggests it. The tradition concurs that this goal represents a qualitatively new and different state of being, which in Scripture is described as incorporation into Christ, or into God through Christ. Pauline thought articulates the goal in terms of a contrast posed between the old man (symbolized by Adam) and the new man (who is Christ). The classic text is Paul's statement that if anyone is in Christ, he or she is a new creation (2 Cor. 5:17). It is utterly clear that this state represents a movement away from what we were, initially, toward the goal of the human drive of transcendence. It is thus a mode of transformation, and the way to it requires significant change in the person. The term *conversion* is used to signify the process that, if it is to achieve the goal, must be lifelong.[12]

Another reason for the use of the term *conversion* is that important modern commentators within the Christian tradition have chosen it to discuss the process of religious maturation. Two who have selected it as their term are William James and Donald Gelpi, and it is their work that will be offered as examples of strong paradigms dealing with the problems of developing an authentic religious conscience. Thus it is appropriate to present their positions in their language.

William James was an original and early commentator in America who described, among the wide spectrum of religious experiences, the special place that conversion occupies. From his fascinating testimonies of individual experiences, he selected those elements that he perceived as crucial components. Analyzing the ordinary states of consciousness in human life as alternating and transitory, he works to a definition of the self as divided. On certain occasions one concern grows so stable as to expel its rivals, and when that happens, we recognize a transformation.[13] What causes such transformation is the way in which emotional excitement changes, so that things that are "hot" and "vital" (James's terms) to us today are cold tomorrow.[14] A significant shift occurs when the focus of heat (from the standpoint of the person) establishes itself permanently within a certain system. If the change is a religious one, we denote it by the term *conversion*. (For James, a sure clue to recognizing it as such is its arrival after a crisis.)[15] He goes on to carefully define the language used, so that the hot place in one's consciousness is explained as the group of ideas to which one devotes oneself and from which one works (i.e., the habitual center of one's personal energy). And James asserts that it makes a very great difference which set of ideas centers one's energy. To say that a person is "converted" means that religious ideas, previously peripheral in consciousness, now assume a central place, and that religious aims form the habitual center of energy.[16] *How* this happens was for James and the psychology of his day a mystery.

From another aspect, James offers some provocative thoughts on the significance of conversion in human development. Acknowledging his debt to Professor Starbuck, James suggests that youthful conversion is part of the normal process in the child's passages from a small universe to the wider intellectual and spiritual life of maturity. But conversion intensifies this period and shortens it by bringing the person to a definite crisis.[17]

Referring to another authority on the psychology of conversion, Professor Leuba, he expands the discussion by focusing on the moral aspect. The religious sense here is one of conviction of sin and a feeling of unwholeness, both of which urge the person to seek relief. Though he critiques the exclusive use of this dimension as too narrow, James incorporates a profound moral regeneration as part of the conversion process. Then he proceeds to describe two types of conversion: volitional and that of self-surrender. In the first, the regeneration is usually gradual and is achieved by building up, piece by piece, a new set of moral and spiritual habits. The self-surrender type occurs when the personal will has done everything possible and still it is not enough. The last step must be left to other forces, and this necessitates a surrender of personal will. An acute analysis of the appropriateness and necessity of such a step follows.

For most, the state of present incompleteness is one from which we are eager to escape, yet the positive goal toward which we are striving is only dimly imagined, since it is not yet ours to know. Moreover, the personal will is part of the problem of sin, and it must be relinquished. The result is a situation of profound extremity and helplessness. Thus, we reach for the power of redemption, which is perceived as beyond us.[18] This second model emphasizes the rare and more drastic shift of consciousness, and it is included here because it so clearly illuminates the totality of the change that is an essential part of the conversion process, in a way that stresses the emotional price that is paid for it.

Perhaps one of the most interesting conclusions James draws follows his recounting of several stories of instantaneous conversion. On the surface and even on the conscious level of the experiencing subject, these appear miraculous, an intervention from beyond that seizes the person and brings him or her to a place long desired but considered unattainable. James carefully states the limits of his field of inquiry and proceeds to examine them on their psychological side, exclusively. What seems to produce these conversions is a simple psychological peculiarity; namely, in these subjects we find persons who are in possession of a large field of consciousness in which mental work can go on subliminally, and from which invasive experiences may enter to upset the equilibrium of the primary consciousness.[19] This is *not* a derogatory remark for James, for whom the origin of something was infinitely less interesting than its fruits. And it raises some very interesting theories about the cognitive environment in which religious regeneration can occur. For James argues here that moments of conversion are part of an extended process that admits of degrees of intensity and awareness, yet all of its stages are important for the achievement of a renewed life.

Finally, James stresses that the fruits of conversion lie in the realm of moral regeneration. The real witness of the spirit to conversion is found only in the disposition of a genuine child of God in which the telling characteristics are a permanently patient heart, and one in which the love of self has been eradicated. This state is *not* a special one, at variance with natural development, but rather part of the continuum of human progress in excellence and moral goodness.[20] By thus dissolving the barrier between nature and supernature, James has rendered the inestimable service of placing the event of conversion in the center of human life as it evolves intellectually, morally, and spiritually. In his analysis we can begin to see the shape of a contemporary understanding of the process of conversion, which acknowledges that attention must be paid to every facet of psychological and social development if conversion is to occur as a necessary part of religious living in the world today. At this point, it is essential to emphasize that, although James is most well known for his analyses of drastic shifts of religious awareness, he clearly saw that the religious life as a whole must be subject to continual growth and change in the direction of greater clarity of vision and intensity of will.

A contemporary model of Christian conversion has been offered by the Berkeley theologian Donald Gelpi. In his book, *Charism and Sacrament,* Father Gelpi explores an experiential theology of conversion in an attempt to contextualize the abundant flowering of transforming experiences fostered by the charismatic renewal. As it stands, his book presents rich insights into the process of conversion as a necessary part of the development of Christian maturity. In the time since James wrote his reflections, discoveries in psychology have added greater shades of precision to any investigation of religious experience. Gelpi acknowledges this at the start by stating that conversion to God is a complex human process. He distinguishes four kinds of graces that are apparent within conversion to God: environmental, emotive, inferential, and decisive. Environmental grace is an event that is spirit-inspired and that calls a person to acknowledge God's presence and action. Along with salvific facts are those events that occur through a direct action of the spirit on the human heart. This first grace is, however, just the beginning; it is a call that invites a number of different perceptions and responses, and among these the emotive response ranks high. Conversion is not only (or even primarily) a matter of the intellect, but of the heart. The third grace, which he designates as inferential grace, involves critical reformulation of a person's religious creed. The fourth grace rests in the area of decision, where faith manifests its life in acts of love and service.

Gelpi's point is that all of these movements are necessary, that in a genuine religious conversion, one assumes personal responsibility for responding in an appropriate way to every impulse of divine grace. This entails responses on the emotive, inferential, and decisional levels, and so mandates that we assume responsibility for our emotional, speculative, and practical growth. Logic tells us that disordered emotional attitudes, false and inadequate beliefs, and disordered patterns of activity present obstacles to proper response to the spirit's saving action and environmental graces. Gelpi vividly reminds us of valuable insights present in the spiritual teaching of the Christian tradition. Emotional obstacles are the cause of blindness. Some eminent examples of this power are the emotions of anger, guilt, fear, resentment, and hatred. These produce severe distortions of knowledge of self and others and effectively hamper recognition of our need for God. False and inadequate beliefs are another cause of blindness in this instance on the speculative level. Gelpi locates the root of this form of blindness in the fact that we perceive things concretely, but grasp their meaning inferentially. This opens the possibility that we see without seeing. (Parenthetically, let us note here that speculative blindness is a major cause of social injustice, and its eradication is a perennial problem to the spiritual leaders of any community.)

If disordered feelings and shortsighted views blind us, disordered decisions and attachments chain us. God's will regarding our failures may be perfectly clear to us, but we will still refuse to surrender to it because we choose to remain complacent and attached to some person or thing. For example, greed or lust can hold us so powerfully that nothing short of Paul's experience on the Damascus road could succeed in moving us to turn to God.

From this perspective, the conversion process is not only religious, but involves affective, intellectual, and moral conversion. Such a transformation is awesome to consider, yet the Christian tradition affirms that it can take place if God's grace and human effort cooperate. The initiation of the process comes from God's side in the form of divine grace. Without that impulse and supporting help throughout, the process could never succeed, for human effort could not sustain it. By the same token, human effort is the essential ingredient on the personal level, for here the individual shows the willingness to respond and thus manifests good faith. What can be accomplished by human effort in terms of intellectual, moral, and affective conversion contributes essentially to the conversion process. Two examples indicate the basic and concrete efforts that Gelpi postulates. Human anguish stemming from unacknowledged anger, fear, and guilt can bring a person to recognize the need for professional psychological help. Awakening to one's selfishness can evoke shame and the desire to resolve to make only responsible moral decisions that respond appropriately to one's environment.

The common thread in all these stages of conversion is the decision to take personal responsibility for the development of a given aspect of our experience. Yet the total picture of conversion shows that an integral and authentic transformation is fourfold and involves four distinct kinds of interrelated decisions. The practical implication of this is that a person can enter the process at any one of the four levels. Beginning on the intellectual level, one can move on to religious, affective, and moral conversion. Or one could begin on the moral level and then proceed to the other stages. Any conversion that remains only on one level is unauthentic, and unauthenticity in this complex process is capable of eroding one's initial commitment. The reason is simple: all the stages require each other for perfection. If the moral commitment is not shaped by the intellectual, it will easily break down and run the double danger of falling into entropy or becoming radically mistaken. On another level, the morally converted individual claims to have taken a stance regarding authentic values. That standpoint cannot be whole without knowledge of the religious values that are an essential part of what humanity regards as worthy of pursuit and respect. Furthermore, the ethically converted person who is aesthetically unconverted can turn into the type of insensitive individual who is unaware of the harm he or she does to others.

Ideally, then, the process of conversion will move from an initial breakthrough on one of these levels and proceed to the others. The minimum requisite is that openness to further development is present in the initial stage and is maintained throughout the entire process. Thus Gelpi gives a modern and psychologically informed reading of the long-standing Christian conviction that conversion is an ongoing, lifelong process that has as its goal the transformation of the human person seen as an integral, complex being with many levels of meaning.[21]

The success of this model in dealing with the transmission of concern regarding social justice is immediately apparent in his following chapter on the mind of Jesus. Discussing it will help to focus the insights gained from both examples into practical implications for contemporary religious formation in social justice. For the fundamental gift any tradition has to offer is its concept of the sacred and the way in which it interacts with the world of our being and acting. It provides the model through which a tradition communicates its best wisdom and lessons for life. In Christianity Jesus has always been the exemplar and the mediator between God and humanity. If we would seek to know what the goal of Christian conversion means, we must look to him. Gelpi selects from the rich variety of images in the New Testament those he believes speaks to the needs of the contemporary Christian who is called to live in a world of complex tensions (perhaps the severest of these are to be found precisely in the issues raised by poverty and injustice). From the temptation scene, Gelpi draws the essential theme of Jesus' rejection of the lure to test God, and his acceptance of a posture of unconditional commitment to the Father. Applied to the individual in the context of a covenant religion, this commitment finds expression in the unconditional character of one's commitment to others in the name of God. Concretely, this mutual commitment takes the form of community sharing—a type of sharing that is based on faith and is unrestricted by nature. This practical, gratuitous sharing of good is the means by which an authentic child of God mediates atonement; thus it should be an expression of mutual reconciliation in love. It is precisely this form of love that has gained the recognition of a distinctively Christian love.[22]

This image of Jesus has emerged as the foundation for much of the moral teaching of the official magisterium's pastoral statements. Although these advocate the communal sharing of the New Testament with the recognition that personal sacrifice is always in some way a part of that sharing, they condemn unequivocally the presence of widespread economic destitution as an offense in God's sight. Such destitution is a severe injustice, for it always entails human degradation, and it is sin because it is an abuse and exploitation of other persons. The separation of society into haves and have-nots is, therefore, the visible social expression of the absence of authentic religious conversion. Thus, the call to Christians is to oppose actively and prophetically those structures in society and in international exchanges that reflect greed and social and political exploitation.[23] There is no choice, for to ignore the need and condone the causes is to remain within an unregenerate state in which the vision has been obscured, the sensitivity dulled, and the will enervated. Such a state is the absolute contradiction of what Scripture and tradition affirm is the mind and will of God for all his creation. It is the polar opposite of the goal of Christian transformation.

James aptly stresses the role of conversion in total human development, and his thought converges with that of Gelpi when he speaks of the need to take into account the subliminal impulses and subconscious strivings for liberation and growth to maturity. He stresses that the moment of religious conversion partakes of an intricate process of psychic development and is influenced by many factors in our inner life as well as in our outer environment. Furthermore, he characterizes the conversion process as one dynamism in the movement of the adolescent or undeveloped individual, from the sphere of self-centeredness to responsible citizenship in the larger community.

Conversion for both James and Gelpi represents a process of profound human transformations of which the goal is an individual at home with self, world, and God—conscious, loving, and free. Both authors carefully stress the exalted nature of this ideal, but at the same time urge that it is crucial to becoming fully human. What they both offer is an understanding of the task before the Christian tradition (as one among many ways of salvation) as it strives to convey the ideals and its passionate concern in a way that connects with the needs of the contemporary human scene. Person and world are united in the Christian vision in a deeply involving relationship, and that leads the tradition to affirm today that the perennial goal of religion must be clearly defined in terms of that relationship. Personal transformation is inadequate without the perception and the conviction it inspires that the social dimensions of it must receive equal attention. In this case, ignorance of that crucial bond is still the best name for sin. Moreover, contemporary spirituality has recaptured the sense that the individual call to this commitment most fittingly finds expression in a community that shares a vision and offers mutual support to those who struggle to achieve it.

This chapter was written to highlight the connection between spirituality and justice, in the conviction that the problem of religion in the complex relationship of rich and poor nations must never forget that the huge effort needed to renew the face of the earth demands for its achievement profound measures of human transformation. For such changes, the religious institutions must prepare those who will be the hands and voice of the compassionate and just God. It is not enough to consider the task accomplished in the raising up of a few dynamic, committed leaders. Changes in the social order touch each member of the human community, and resistance in any sector can effectively block the change. Nor is the task finished in the work of one generation. The vision of a world where suffering is reduced and injustice shackled urges each religion to deeply concern itself with the ongoing transformation of its members. This chapter has presented some contemporary Christian thinking on this challenge.

NOTES

1. Helder Camara, "The First World Is the Problem," *Cross Currents,* no. 2 (Summer 1970): 258–62.
2. John C. Haughey, ed., *The Faith That Does Justice* (New York: Paulist Press, 1977), 207.
3. Choan-Seng Song, *Third-Eye Theology* (Maryknoll, NY: Orbis Press, 1979), 63.
4. Ibid., 64.
5. Ibid., 67–68.
6. Daniel Maguire, "The Primary of Justice in Moral Theology," *Horizons* 10, no. 1 (Spring 1983): 74.

7. Ibid., 76.
8. Matthew Lamb, "Christian Spirituality and Social Justice," *Horizons* 10, no. 1 (Spring 1983): 34.
9. Ibid., 34–35.
10. Alexis de Toqueville, *Democracy in America,* trans. Henry Reeve, edited by Phillips Bradley, 2 vols. (New York: Alfred A. Knopf, 1953), 2:23.
11. Lamb, 45–49.
12. Though this term has been discussed in the context of the Christian tradition, it is clear that, in its fullest meaning, it has universal application.
13. William James, *The Varieties of Religious Experience* (New York: New American Library/Mentor, 1958), 160.
14. Ibid., 161.
15. Ibid., 162.
16. Ibid.
17. Ibid., 164.
18. Ibid., 169–74.
19. Ibid., 190–91.
20. Ibid., 192.
21. Donald L. Gelpi, *Charism and Sacrament: A Theology of Christian Conversion* (New York: Paulist, 1976), 15–21.
22. Ibid., 35.
23. Ibid., 41–42.

Part Two
RICH AND POOR NATIONS

5
Religion and Economic Development

ELLEN H. PALANCA

In theories of economic development, economic factors such as human resources, natural resources, capital accumulation, and technology form the core of the analysis. Noneconomic factors such as politics, culture, religion, ideology, and institutions are treated as part of the background setting and are usually not included. However, in most instances of development, a favorable noneconomic factor is necessarily present to provide the motivation and/or the proper institutional setting. Politics, religion, or secular ideology usually provides this.

Very few economists take an interdisciplinary approach in the research and analysis of economic conditions. Noneconomic factors usually are not included in economic analysis, as they are difficult to quantify and are less subject to change. Religion and culture are almost impossible to change, although they do transform with social change. Change in politics and ideology is usually the result of a change in the ruling class or of a violent revolution. Even the evolution of institutions involves a long, painful process. However, the importance of these variables as constituting the basic framework in development studies cannot be neglected. In his textbook on basic economics, intended for use in Third World countries, Michael Todaro makes the following caution:

> The achievement of development and the solution to development problems is a much more complicated task than some economists would lead us to believe. Increasing national production, raising levels of living and promoting widespread employment opportunities are as much a function of the values, incentives, attitudes and beliefs, and the institutional and power arrangements of a society, as they are the direct outcomes of the manipulation of strategic economic variables such as savings, investment and export.

Religion and Per Capita Income: Empirical Data

In this essay we examine one noneconomic factor—religion—and see how it can affect economic development. The influence of religion on economic development gained attention with Max Weber's well-known Protestant ethic thesis, which attributes the development of capitalism to the influence of Protestantism. Although this thesis has caused debate among social scientists, its impact on the social sciences, particularly in analyzing economic development and social progress, has remained strong. The general contention has been that there is a certain degree of validity to Weber's hypothesis. Development economists have recognized the role religion plays in the development, of nations.

In his book on economic development, Higgins observes a relationship between predominant religion and per capita income, which he says is "too close for religion to be dismissed out of hand as a factor in past economic history." Using per capita income figures for 1961 (see Table 1, page 76), Higgins shows that

> "the six countries with the highest per capita incomes in 1961 are Christian and Protestant. Of the twenty-two countries with per capita incomes over $600 per year (the "developed" countries in our definition), all but seven are predominantly Protestant, the others (except Israel) are predominantly Roman Catholic. Those with per capita incomes between $250 and $600 are mainly Roman Catholic; those between $100 and $250 are mainly Roman Catholic and Moslem; those below $100 are mainly Hindu, Buddhist, and pagan."

The same information for 1981 is presented by Higgins in Table 2 (see page 79). The table presents the predominant religion of the countries. The same general pattern of relationship between religion and per capita income can be observed. Among those countries with very high per capita incomes (over $7000), excluding the oil exporters, most (13 out of 17) of these advanced countries are Protestant. Roman Catholicism is the religion for many of the high middle-income countries ($2000 to $7000). The low middle-income countries ($500 to $2000) are mostly Roman Catholic and Moslem. For the countries with very low per capita incomes (below $500), we observe that Islam, Buddhism, Hinduism, and African tribal religions are the predominant religions.

It is interesting to note the diverse religious backgrounds among the top high middle-income countries (countries with per capita income between $4000 and $7000). In general, most of the religions in this group are Christian (Roman Catholic, Orthodox Christian, and Protestant). However, we also have in this group some notable exceptions, namely, Israel, Singapore, and Hong Kong. Israel is also high on the list in Table 1 (page 0). In fact Judaism was believed to have been the primary source of the spirit of capitalism by Sombart, who conceived of the concept of "spirit of capitalism."[1] In the case of Singapore and Hong Kong, Confucian teaching provides an economic ethic conducive to perseverance and accumulation. Whatever their religion, most Chinese are influenced by Confucianism. The same explanation applies to the economic success of Chinese in the Southeast Asian countries.

There is a general pattern between economic development and religion. This general pattern cannot be definite, conclusive evidence of a cause and effect relationship. However, it does indicate that religion is a factor, if not the cause, of economic growth. Moreover, the relationship between religion and growth is perhaps not a one-way causal relationship but a reciprocal one, as there seems to be a constant interaction between the two realms. Religion is a factor of growth to the extent that it stimulates economic activities and evinces transformative change in the societal and economic structures in turn, contributing to development and progress. On the other hand, religion is not static but transforms with time as it is affected by social and economic development. Social environment and economic conditions influence the development of religious attitudes. One can compare the traditional and modern forms of any religion to realize how it has adapted to modern situations. Usually the religions which evince change are also the ones which adapt faster to change. Such a two-way relationship between religion and development was recognized by Tawney.[2] He believed that the Protestant ethic had contributed to the rise in capitalism but at the same time Protestantism itself was being influenced by an increasingly capitalistic society. In this way Tawney differed from Weber, who gave primacy to the spiritual factors.

Motivational and Transformative Effects of Religion

In a non-Communist economy the increase in the national productive capacity is the result of work effort and the utilization of economic opportunities by individuals for material advancement. The sum total of such individual effect produces national economic growth. In many cases in history, external factors such as foreign capital or trade provided economic opportunities, stimulated economic activities, and even brought about social and cultural changes. It has been explained that the Protestant Reformation could have the result of economic opportunities provided by the geographical discoveries in the fifteenth and sixteenth centuries. At any rate, growth and development can take place only if there are motivation for more work effort and the necessary institutional transformation conducive for development. For individuals, the variation in income and wealth cannot be explained solely by the amount of work exerted. Ability, connections, luck, chance, and windfalls are also explanatory factors of economic success. However, for society as a whole, unless its resource endowment is exceptional, economic development is the result of work and entrepreneurial ventures.

How does a religion affect development? What are the mechanisms involved? What characteristics of a religion determine the extent of relationship it has with the development of the country, particularly its economy? These are some questions which social scientists have addressed in the investigation of the relationship between religion and economic development.

The process by which religion affects development involves both motivational as well as institutional factors. Weber's thesis argues that by the motivational approach, economic growth is stimulated by the economic ethic provided by a religion to the extent that it embodies achievement motivation. Weber believes that the Protestant ethic encourages entrepreneurial activities and accumulation of wealth. The other effect or mechanism by which religion affects development is through its institutional transformation capacities. By this institutional approach, it is meant that religion, through its effect on culture, behavior, and mode of doing things, transforms the basic social and economic structures to a form necessary for development.

Both motivation and structural change are important factors in the development of countries. Development economists have recently put due emphasis on these factors. Proper attitudes such as "the desire and ability to modernize, the exaltation of individual self-interest, the motivation for material advancement, the quest for efficiency, etc.,"[3] and important institutions such as "effective tax and credit systems, well-functioning, efficient and incorruptible bureaucratic and administrative structures, functional and relevant educational systems, the legal and cultural sanctity of private property, close linkages between various economic sectors, etc.,"[4] are necessary to put available resources to full use. In Third World countries, the problem usually lies in the deficiency of such favorable institutional and attitudinal prerequisites rather than in resource availability. Perhaps the most pronounced resource deficiency usually cited is capital. However, the generation and accumulation of capital depend a great deal on the motivation to earn and save and the institutional framework of the economy.

The motivational factors of religion are strongly emphasized in Weber's concept. From Weber's analysis we can gather and summarize that the motivation to economic activities was enhanced by the ethic code of Protestantism through its emphasis on: 1) work as a way of life, 2) worldly asceticism, and 3) rationalism.

Protestantism teaches that work is a calling; hence the pursuit of wealth is justified. In fact, following the ethic, an individual is made to feel that he or she has the moral duty and obligation to make money. A worker has the duty to make money, not just enough for the provisions of his or her family, but to work in order to make as much money as possible. A merchant should also do the most and best he or she can in carrying on commercial activities. Income and profits earned from such activities, as long as they are honestly earned, are justified and encouraged. This attitude towards work and sense of responsibility to earn money are absent in some low-income countries. In a study on labor supply in an African country, it is observed that farm workers tend to work only for a certain income level which is just enough to sustain themselves and their families.[5] Hence they tend to decrease work hours when offered a higher wage rate. Given such a work force, it is difficult to increase the production of the economy. In a modern society where people are attracted to all sorts of consumer products and services, motivating them to work is less of a problem. Work as a way of life is generally accepted. This is in contrast to what Weber calls traditionalism, which condemned not only usury but any form of profitable activity. Medieval Christianity considered the merchant's calling or merchant's work an occupation that was incompatible with religious and pious living.

How does this ethic encourage capital formation? Capitalism cannot develop without people accumulating capital, i.e., saving part of what they earn. Honest money earning is not sufficient. The ethic obliges people not only to work to their fullest capability and make as much money as possible, but also to save the money and place it in productive investments. Indulgence and frivolous consumption are discouraged. This worldly asceticism leads to entrepreneurial activities and accumulation of wealth and capital.

We see that Protestantism exalts diligence and condemns idleness; it exalts saving and condemns spending. Weber indicates that what happened in history was that the effect of this ethic extended to all other aspects of life. Christian values were applied to secular matters. Hence a new kind of middle-class morality and value system which stressed honesty, frugality, punctuality, risk bearing, and equality of opportunity developed. In this way more work and more goal-oriented individuals developed.

This Protestant attitude toward business and work is what Weber called rationalism, i.e., the careful, planned, and calculated way of doing things. Weber believed that economic development was the result of having this rationalism applied to all aspects of life as well as throughout the social and economic system. This rationalism enhanced the development of knowledge and institutions which were necessary for development.

The motivation for achievement as a cause for economic development has been strongly expounded by David McClelland, a psychologist interested in economic matters. McClelland's hypothesis states that "a society with a generally high level of achievement will produce more energetic entrepreneurs who, in turn, produce more rapid economic development."[6] Motivation for achievement through religion is considered merely as a special case. For groups of people, high need achievement may have been caused by failure factors, for example, defeat in a war or being persecuted (as with a minority group). The remarkable rehabilitation of Japan and Germany after World War II and the economic success cases of Taiwan, the Jews and the Southeast Asian Chinese may also be explained by such factors. We have mentioned that the discipline of the Jews as well as the Southeast Asian Chinese is similar to that of the Protestant ethic. In fact, the motivational factors used to explain these minority groups had also been used to explain the impact of Protestantism on success, as the Protestants in the seventeenth century were also a minority group, although not as persecuted a group. Of course, not all religious minority groups do better than the majority groups. Notable exceptions are the Catholics in Canada and the Moslems in India and the Philippines.

Another important impact of religion on development is its effect on the basic social and economic structure of the country. A few critics of Weber questioned the direct motivational effect of the Protestant ethic which Weber strongly stressed; instead, they maintained that the effect Protestantism had on modernization was made indirectly through its transformative capacities on the structures of society. The Protestant attitude in doing things is extended to all aspects of human life. The rationalism of Protestantism led to the development of new patterns of human relationships, the construction of new organizations, and the institutionalization of education, law, science, and technology. Hence, the effect of Protestant Reformation was not only on its economy but also on its legal system, its political structure, and also all fields of knowledge. The more efficient and impersonal system gave way to the old system. The moral values and attitudes inculcated by the ethic were widespread, as there was a tendency for its mystical contemplation to be secularized. This rationalism developed a middle-class morality which was the basis by which people related to each other. This kind of relationship led to more willingness to trade with strangers and hence the development of contractual relationships. Economic relations expanded as they moved increasingly to a more impersonal basis. Other institutions, such as the use of money and the organization of marketing and finance, also developed. Producing organizations became more complex and large scale. The search for knowledge through empiricism developed institutionalized science and technology as well as the education system. All these together led to more liberalized institutions which facilitated more work effort and accumulation.

We see therefore that there is an interaction between institutions and development. New and favorable institutions promote development, and at the same time they became more liberalized as development takes place. It is this interaction which makes it difficult for social scientists to determine whether the Protestant Reformation was the result of economic opportunities, or if theological changes led to economic changes.

The motivational approach and institutional approach of religious impact are also closely related. On the motivational level, a religion which motivates does not only stimulate entrepreneurial activities but also stimulates the motivation to undertake other types of nonreligious roles. This leads to the development and improvement of secular institutions. However, this does not always happen. It happened with the Protestant ethic but did not happen with Confucianism. On the other hand, economic development also depends very much on the institutional channeling of motivation. For a country with a poor credit system and inefficient government, even with the presence of people with entrepreneurial inclinations, economic activities would still be at a minimum. Without the right setting, these people could not develop their potential. Confucianism, although not really a religion, in that it does not have a transcendental God, provides an economic ethic that emphasizes accumulation and thrift. Confucianism teaches that accumulation of wealth is one sure way to ensure that one's parents will be comfortable. However, "the familial piety inculcated by Confucianism hindered the development of the impersonal economic ethic so necessary to rational calculation in business affairs"[7] Another reason why development did not take place in China for a long time was the overprotection of the literati stratum of society and the low social status of businessmen. In the order of importance in society, the literati occupied the highest order, followed by the farmers and artisans, with merchants occupying the lowest stratum. Hence, without a favorable environment in which to operate, many of the merchants migrated to other nearby countries and have been doing well for several generations.

We have seen how the direct economic ethic embodied in a given religion can influence the attitude of the religion's followers toward business. Other aspects of its religious ethic such as its transcendentalism, the extent of its third-world orientation, and its social openness also affect its motivation and transformative capacities. All religions talk about a life after death. However, some religions concentrate only on the next life and neglect the present life. The next life is anticipated with the hope that it will compensate for whatever pains and hardships one suffers at present. An appropriate example is the case of Hinduism, where the promise of reincarnation into a higher caste is reward for keeping dutifully to one's station in life. It is difficult to imagine people with such a fatalistic attitude and lack of a work ethic. For people with strong other-world orientation, asceticism and accumulation concerning this-world material things are not emphasized.

Traditional religions which transform in order to adapt to modern times necessarily become more this-world oriented. Traditionally, the religious values of Buddhism put emphasis on the purification of human character and do not emphasize the material goal of society. However, Ames believes that Buddhism in Ceylon (now Sri Lanka) went through a reformation which has brought about orientations supporting social reforms. Comparing traditional Buddhism and modern Buddhism, Ames said:

> Modern Buddhists are more achievement-oriented than are their rural counterparts. Because salvation is felt to be closer or more immediate, reformers feel less need to pay attention to the round of rebirths and the many Buddhist pinkama rituals concerned with improving one's rebirth chances. It is how one performs here and now, in this life itself, that really counts.[8]

The other effect or mechanism by which religion affects its development is through its structural transformation capacities. Eisenstadt discusses the determinants of the transformative capacities of religions or ideological movements.[9] The same characteristics of openness, transcendentalism, and this-worldliness also define the transformative effect of a religion. A more this-world oriented religion has more commitment to and involvement in activities in the secular world. Such an involvement is more likely to bring about innovation or change in the institutions (cultural, juridical, legislative, economic) necessary for development. Conversely, the more other-worldly activists tendencies within a religious value system are, the less likely they would orient themselves to the structural reformation of society, thus lessening their impact on the institutional structures of the country.

One characteristic of religion which Eisenstadt believes is important in the determination of its transformation generating capacity is the degree of organizational autonomy of the religion in the country. The more autonomous the religious organizations are, the greater is their capacity to develop new political and cultural symbols or any system of reforms. In Islamic countries there is a very close identity between politics and religion. This lack of autonomy greatly suppresses transformation movements in these countries. (Weber used this as an example of a religion which has been inhibited in initiating reform movements.)

It has also been mentioned that in some cases historical circumstances which provided a psychological need to achieve might have contributed more to motivating accumulation than a religious ethic alone. Moreover, other factors which fulfill the functions of providing proper motivation and appropriate institutional frameworks can also generate the necessary environment for growth to start. We have seen in more recent history the emergence of a few economically successful cases which are results of strong and responsible governments that cater to such developmental needs.

How do we apply these speculations of the relationship between religion and development to the situations of developing countries today? More specifically, how can we hasten the development process of the Philippines? There is no way that a certain religious ethic can be imposed. Besides, in most countries today, with the decreasing role of religion and the church in society, we cannot expect a religious ethic to play as important a role as it did in the medieval times and during the Reformation.

In most developing countries today the psychological need to strive for material well-being is present. Like the people in the advanced countries, people in the developing countries do have the motivation to earn money. In fact, many people are guided by such a motivation in many of the decisions which they make. Some negative effect on such motivation is usually put on the extended family system. In such a system, a person does not actually enjoy all the fruit of his labor because most of it has to be shared with relatives and perhaps a whole clan. The dependents are also less motivated to work and earn money, as the need is not that immediate. However, institutions do change with progress. The extended family system is no longer as prevalent as before, and small nuclear families have taken its place.

In general, we see that most people do have the desire to work and make money. In fact, whether desirable or not, with the influence of Western culture, for many people such a desire determines their lives and thinking. However, does the system encourage work in the sense that work is justly rewarded? Or do people who have power, economic or political, and the right connection get better rewarded? Does the system encourage people to seek economic opportunities? Can an ordinary person who sees opportunity in an agricultural crop simply venture into it? Will an individual be able to get the credit that is needed, and can he or she easily make use of the system for marketing a product? Can a person with no connections whatsoever, who sees opportunity in manufacturing, enter into the market without encountering barriers in finance and distribution created by monopolistic elements? Such motivational problems are due to the lack of favorable institutions for entrepreneurship, rather than the lack of motivation on a psychological level.

Without the generation of income, the generation of capital is impossible. If labor provided by the unskilled and semi-skilled laborers is not sufficiently rewarded, then such laborers will not be encouraged to work. Those who do work earn very low incomes. Many people live below the poverty line and most people have only subsistence incomes. Hence we can only talk of generating wealth and savings from the rich. For this group of people there are many attractions to the imported luxury items; hence saving is low. Moreover, the investment done by this group of people is mostly in the nonproductive and passive type of investments. The system is such that this type of investment is more rewarding than the productive type of investment. The risks and difficulties of starting a new business are numerous, while it is easier and safer to speculate on land and jewelry. For those who do go into productive economic ventures, some confront more odds than others as the system practices favoritism, meaning that some prosper while others do not. The government has launched several projects aimed at helping the low income people to venture into small scale businesses. However, so far these have not succeeded in increasing the welfare of the public but have only succeeded in increasing the power and degree of bureaucracy of the government.

The rise of Japan after World War II, and later the impressive growth of Singapore, Korea, Taiwan, and Hong Kong have demonstrated the importance of the government in providing favorable institutional mechanisms for saving and investment. Singapore has practically no resources except human resources. However, through its strong and responsible government it has enjoyed a high and stable growth rate and also a very low inflation rate. The government has in effect fulfilled the functions of providing incentives and institutions necessary for development. These functions are believed to have been provided by Protestantism in the development of capitalism, which is similar to the explanation of growth in many countries in Europe and North America.

NOTES

1. Michael Todaro, *Economics for a Developing World* (London: Longman Group Limited, 1977), 23.
2. Max Weber, *The Protestant Ethic and the Spirit of Capitalism* (New York: Scribner, 1968).

3. Benjamin Higgins, *Economic Development* (New York: W. W. Norton & Co., Inc., 1968), 165.
4. *Ibid.*
5. Robert Green, "Introduction" *Protestantism, Capitalism and Social Science* ed. Robert Green, (Massachusetts: D. C. Heath & Co., 1973), xi.
6. Richard Tawney, *Religion and the Rise of Capitalism* (New York: Harcourt, 1962).
7. Michael Todaro, *Economics for a Developing World* (London: Longman Group Limited, 1977), 62.
8. *Ibid.*
9. E. J. Berg, "Backward-Sloping Labor Supply Functions in Dual Economies—the Africa Case," *Quarterly Journal of Economics,* 1961.
10. David McClelland, *The Achieving Society* (Princeton: Princeton University Press, 1962), 205.
11. R. Stephen Warner, "Weber's Sociology of Nonwestern Religions," in *Protestantism, Capitalism, and Social Science* ed. Robert Green, (Massachusetts: D. C. Heath & Co., 1973), 37.
12. Michael Ames, "Ideological and Social Change in Ceylon," *Human Organization,* XXII, No. 1963, p. 48; also in S. N. Eisenstadt, ed., *The Protestant Ethic and Modernization* (New York: Basic Books, Inc., 1968), 271–88.
13. S. N. Eisenstadt, "The Protestant Ethic Thesis in an Analytical and Comparative Framework" in S. N. Eisenstadt, ed., *The Protestant Ethic and Modernization,* 3–45.

TABLE 1

Gross National Product per Capita, 1961
(in U.S. dollars)

Country	*GNP per capita*
Over $2,000	
United States	$2,790
Canada	2,048
$1,000 to $2,000	
Sweden	1,557
Switzerland	1,555
Australia	1,475
New Zealand	1,470
Belgium	1,348
Great Britain	1,345
Norway	1,223
France	1,203
Denmark	1,193

TABLE 1 (continued)

Gross National Product per Capita, 1961
(in U.S. dollars)

Country	*GNP per capita*
$1,000 to $2,000	
West Germany	1,113
$500 to $1,000	
Netherlands	954
Finland	893
Austria	830
Soviet Union	818
Israel	733
East Germany	700
Czechoslovakia	650
Venezuela	644
Puerto Rico	643
Italy	623
Ireland	570
Argentina	533
$250 to $500	
Hungary	475
Uruguay	449
Bulgaria	440
Poland	440
Romania	440
South Africa	427
Cuba	413
Greece	383
Japan	383
Malaya	368
Jamaica	357
Chile	348
Spain	321
Lebanon	319
Yugoslavia	306
Mexico	297
Colombia	287
Panama	283
Costa Rica	278
Brazil	268
Dominican Republic	251

TABLE 1 (continued)

Gross National Product per Capita, 1961
(in U.S. dollars)

Country	GNP per capita
$100 to $250	
Albania	240
Portugal	240
Turkey	222
Nicaragua	206
El Salvador	191
Algeria	190
Philippines	188
Guatemala	184
Honduras	180
Peru	179
Syria	173
Saudi Arabia	170
Iraq	161
Rhodesia and Nyasaland	161
Tunisia	160
Ecuador	159
Egypt	150
Ghana	140
Morocco	140
Paraguay	129
Jordan	126
Ceylon	123
Iran	120
Taiwan	116
South Vietnam	111
South Korea	106
North Korea	105
North Vietnam	105
Thailand	101
Below $100	
Haiti	99
Indonesia	99
Kenya	94
Bolivia	87
Liberia	85
Nigeria	84
China	83
Cambodia	77

TABLE 1 (continued)

Gross National Product per Capita, 1961
(in U.S. dollars)

Country	*GNP per capita*
Below $100	
Ethiopia	76
Sudan	75
Tanganyika	75
India	70
Uganda	66
Pakistan	62
Burma	61
Afghanistan	58
Togoland	55
Laos	52
Nepal	47

Source: Benjamin Higgins, *Economic Development* (New York: W. W. Norton & Co., Inc., 1968).

TABLE 2

Gross National Product per Capita, 1981 and Predominant Religion

Country	*GNP per capita*	*Predominant Religion*
High Income (Over $7000)		
Oil Exporters		
United Arab Emirates	$26,000	Islam
Kuwait	19,830	Islam
Saudi Arabia	11,260	Islam
Libya	8,640	Islam
Others		
Switzerland	16,440	Christianity (50% Protestant) (50% Catholic)
Germany, Fed. Rep.	13,590	Christianity (50% Protestant) (45% Catholic)
Sweden	13,520	Protestantism
Denmark	12,950	Protestantism
Norway	12,650	Protestantism

TABLE 2 (continued)

Gross National Product per Capita, 1981 and Predominant Religion

Country	*GNP per capita*	*Predominant Religion*
Others		
Belgium	12,180	Roman Catholicism
France	11,730	Roman Catholicism
Netherlands	11,470	Protestantism
United States	11,360	Protestantism
Austria	10,230	Roman Catholicism
Canada	10,130	Christianity (45% Protestant) (40% Catholic)
Japan	9,890	Shintoism
Australia	9,820	Protestantism
Finland	9,720	Protestantism
United Kingdom	7,920	Protestantism
Germany, Dem. Rep.	7,180	Protestantism
New Zealand	7,090	Protestantism
High Middle Income *($2000–$7000)*		
Italy	6,480	Roman Catholicism
Czechoslovakia	5,820	Roman Catholicism
Spain	5,400	Roman Catholicism
Ireland	4,880	Roman Catholicism
USSR	4,550	Orthodoxy
Israel	4,500	Judaism
Singapore	4,430	Buddhism
Greece	4,380	Orthodoxy
Puerto Rico*	••	Roman Catholicism
Trinidad and Tobago	4,370	Protestantism
Hong Kong	4,240	Buddhism
Hungary	4,180	Roman Catholicism
Bulgaria	4,150	Orthodoxy
Poland	3,900	Roman Catholicism
Venezuela	3,630	Roman Catholicism
Iraq	3,020	Islam
Iran	••	Islam
Suriname*	••	Roman Catholicism
Uruguay	2,810	Roman Catholicism
Yugoslavia	2,620	Christianity (40% Orthodox) (32% Catholic)

Religion and Economic Development

Gross National Product per Capita, 1981 and Predominant Religion

Country	GNP per capita	Predominant Religion
High Middle Income (*$2000–$7000*)		
Argentina	2,390	Roman Catholicism
Portugal	2,370	Roman Catholicism
Romania	2,340	Roman Catholicism
South Africa	2,300	Protestantism
Chile	2,150	Roman Catholicism
Mexico	2,090	Roman Catholicism
Brazil	2,050	Roman Catholicism
Low Middle Income ($500–$2000)		
Algeria	1,870	Islam
Costa Rica	1,730	Roman Catholicism
Panama	1,730	Roman Catholicism
Malaysia	1,620	Islam
Korea, Rep. of	1,520	Buddhism
Turkey	1,470	Islam
Lebanon	••	Islam
Jordan	1,420	Islam
Syria Arab Rep.	1,340	Islam
Korea, Dem. Rep.	••	Buddhism
Tunisia	1,310	Islam
Paraguay	1,300	Roman Catholicism
Ecuador	1,270	Roman Catholicism
Colombia	1,180	Roman Catholicism
Dominican Rep.	1,160	Roman Catholicism
Ivory Coast	1,150	African Religions
Guatemala	1,080	Roman Catholicism
Jamaica	1,040	Protestantism
Nigeria	1,010	Roman Catholicism
Peru	930	Roman Catholicism
Albania	••	Islam
Morocco	900	Islam
Congo	900	African Religions and Christianity
Botswana*	••	African Religions
Papua New Guinea	780	Protestantism
Nicaragua	740	Roman Catholicism

TABLE 2 (continued)

Gross National Product per Capita, 1981 and Predominant Religion

Country	*GNP per capita*	*Predominant Religion*
Low Middle Income ($500-$2000)		
Philippines	690	Roman Catholicism
Thailand	670	Buddhism
Cameroon	670	African Religions
El Salvador	660	Roman Catholicism
Zimbabwe	630	African Religions and Christianity
Egypt	580	Islam
Bolivia	570	Roman Catholicism
Honduras	560	Roman Catholicism
Zambia	560	African Religions
Liberia	530	African Religions
Low Income (Below $500)		
Angola	470	African Religions
Senegal	450	Islam
Mauritania	440	Islam
Indonesia	430	Islam
Yemen Arab Rep.	430	Islam
Ghana	420	Roman Catholicism
Kenya	420	African Religions
Lesotho	420	Roman Catholicism
Yemen, PDR	420	Islam
Sudan	410	Islam
Togo	410	African Religions
Madagascar	350	African Religions
Niger	330	Islam
Benin	310	African Religions
Central African Rep.	300	African Religions
Pakistan	300	Islam
Uganda	300	Christianity (30% Protestant) (30% Catholic)
China	290	Buddhism
Guinea	290	Islam
Sierra Leone	280	African Religions
Haiti	270	Roman Catholicism
Sri Lanka	270	Buddhism

TABLE 2 (continued)

Gross National Product per Capita, 1981 and Predominant Religion

Country	*GNP per capita*	*Predominant Religion*
Low Income (Below $500)		
India	240	Hinduism
Malawi	230	African Religions
Mozambique	230	African Religions
Zaire	220	African Religions
Upper Volta	210	African Religions
Burundi	200	African Religions
Rwanda	200	African Religions
Mali	190	Islam
Burma	170	Buddhism
Ethiopia	140	Islam
Nepal	140	Hinduism
Bangladesh	130	Islam
Chad	120	Islam (52%) and African Religions (43%)
Bhutan	80	Buddhism
Lao PDR	••	Buddhism
Kampuchea, Dem.	••	Buddhism

*Not listed in the World Bank report. Relative position is based on position found in the UN Yearbook for 1975 GNP per capita figures.

Source: Income figures are from International Bank for Reconstruction and Development, *World Development Report 1982* (Washington: World Bank, 1982); Information on predominant religion is based on almanacs and encyclopedias.

6

The Relationship Between Development And New Religious Movements in the Tribal Societies of the Third World

HAROLD W. TURNER

Introduction

It is not possible to think of the relationship between rich and poor nations without thinking of modernization and development among the peoples of the Third World. To avoid oversimplification or the equation of development with Westernization it might be better to speak of "social transformation in the spirit of modernity" for "traditional societies" as they are drawn into the mainstream of history where mankind is rapidly "coming of age" in terms of human capacities and responsibilities. However we may speak of these issues, we know there is a large element of social, economic, political, and technical change involved, and also that the high hopes of the last two decades have come to little. Great changes are occurring, but they are seldom those we have planned, and the world development processes stand revealed as bankrupt both of ideas and of power to solve the issues that grow sharper between rich and poor nations. Western economic-growth models and local indigenized socialist models are equally ineffective, apart from some relatively minor successes. The poor become poorer and the rich become richer, and now even the privileged groups see their spin-offs and benefits threatened as civilian governments give way to military dictatorships, followed by a succession of military coups. The World Bank predicts that by 1990 some 70 percent of Africans will be living in what is defined as "absolute poverty," a situation paralleled in much of the rest of the Third World.[1]

The Relevance of Religions

If we try to place the development issue, and all that goes with it, in the context of religion, the problem, if anything, would seem to be increased. To link religions with development is to draw attention to the obstacles these great systems present through their own conservatism, their deep roots, fixed traditions, and institutional inertia. Although roots, traditions, and conservation are essential in religions, what is an asset in this context readily operates as an obstacle when it comes to development in a spirit of modernity. And there is the further and deeper question of whether or not the worldview found in each major religious system is capable of supporting the views of nature, man, time, history, and society that seem integral to modern development.

We may examine this further by looking at what might be accepted as a more favorable example—black Africa, which is rapidly becoming the second great cultural-geographical area in the whole history of Christian expansion. The churches here share the same faith as in Europe, which provided the first great Christian cultural-geographical expansion, and so they share in a worldview that can sustain, and in fact largely created, much of what is meant by the attitudes toward nature, man, and history that are integral to development. And yet the prospect of a religion so equipped being able to maintain and extend the development processes in black Africa is most uncertain. As world pressures force national governments to become ever more stringent and repressive in nations that have no traditions of religious freedom, Christian churches that identify with the needs of the poor, or the weaker tribes and the remoter peoples within a nation, will become increasingly unpopular and subject to restriction by their own governments, and may even be forced into isolation from fellowship with their own religious communities in the outside world.

Missions and churches have undoubtedly been the agents of much basic development in black Africa, as in other parts of the Third World. The church has been the incubator of African nationalism; but since political independence its prophetic role has declined and the new generation of African theologians concentrates on cultural issues rather than on sociopolitical matters, or accepts current policies in their own countries.[2] If the churches are to be faced with increasing frustration in the future, or be driven into silence, where else is there to turn for a new and competent religious dynamic?

It would not be unreasonable at this juncture to examine the great range of new religious movements with which we are all at least vaguely familiar. Indeed, probably no period in history has displayed a greater range and number of religious innovative movements than our own, the so-called "cults and sects" proliferating in the Western world and often generated by interaction between Western and the great Asian traditions. We may turn to these with some anticipation, for they are not yet weighted with the conservatisms and institutions of the older faiths, nor do they easily work in association with governments and so become involved in the concomitant restrictions. Although some of these present a powerful critique of much in Western or other societies and reveal pioneer attempts at developing new life-styles and social forms, few if any would seem to have much relevance to the more obvious meanings of development and modernization as usually understood in the Third World. Although some, such as Baha'i and the Unification Church, have planted roots in Third World countries, I know of no sustained contributions to development at all comparable with those to be detailed in the rest of this chapter.

An Overlooked Range of Religions

I am now drawing attention to a much larger and older range of new religious movements, arising from within the Third World peoples themselves and especially the tribal cultures, but still largely unknown. These have been my special study for over a quarter of a century; I call them simply "new religious movements in primal societies," replacing the rather pejorative and often unacceptable word *tribal* with *primal*. When we look back over the past five centuries we realize that the primal societies of the world have had more extensive and disturbing encounters with the religions and cultures of the higher sophisticated and powerful societies than ever before. Except for Asia and the Islamic areas of North Africa and the Middle East, this has been largely due to the great expansion of the European peoples across the world. On a smaller scale, the tribal peoples marginal to the great Hindu and Buddhist societies of India and Southeast Asia have experienced the renewed impact of these dominant cultures and religions.[3]

In these encounters between small, weak, illiterate primal societies and large, strong, highly organized and literate societies there has been an interaction between two kinds of religion, between the primal or tribal and the kind we call universal. In this interaction, besides total resistance on the one hand and complete conversion on the other, there has been a vast proliferation of new religious movements that owe something both to their own indigenous traditions and to the new invasive religions. Since they are not completely identified with either the old or the new religion, there is usually tension between the new development and both the contributing faiths. This is what I mean by the simple phrase "new religious movements in primal societies." Since movements of this kind have arisen in similar interaction situations across the whole world, with similar features and similar variety of forms, I regard these phenomena as forming a new field in the history of religions, with a worldwide range.

Origins and Forms

Such movements may be found in India, where the scheduled tribes or hill peoples have been responding to their encounter with the Hindu tradition through new religious forms, and in Southeast Asia, where the sophisticated Buddhist cultures of the coastal areas have had the same effect upon the tribal hill peoples of the interior. Similar movements can be identified where Islam has been interacting with the primal religions, chiefly in West Africa and in parts of Indonesia, but there would seem to be fewer examples than could be expected. Since the Hindu and Buddhist interactions have been comparatively restricted in geographical extent and mainly to Asia, the overwhelming proportion of these new religious movements is to be found where Christianity has been the universal religion involved, and this has been largely due to the massive penetration of the tribal world by the modern missionary movement.

The forms taken by these movements are so varied, and the points of view from which they have been described are so diverse, that it is not surprising to find them described by many different names: thus we have prophet, syncretist, messianic, or millennial movements, independent or separatist churches, nativistic or revitalization movements, crisis or deprivation cults, adjustment movements, and the overpublicized and little understood cargo cults of Melanesia. Although some of these terms are appropriate in particular cases, none is suitable as a general term. I therefore use the simple expression "new religious movements," adding "in primal societies" when necessary.

There are three features that distinguish these new religious movements from purely internal developments. The first is the fact that primal religions are nonmissionary, whereas a large proportion of the new movements are distinctly missionary in nature and spread across tribal boundaries. The second feature is the presence of a new kind of eschatology; this goes beyond anything enshrined in the traditional mythology of expectations, which usually promises a return to a paradisal past or golden age rather than the advance to a really new order of existence that has never been conceived before. And finally, these movements serve as a form of adjustment to an exceptionally severe and prolonged traumatic experience from which there is no escape, due to the interaction of two societies that are very disparate in power and sophistication. Each of these features—their universal potential, their innovative capacity, and their adjustments to more developed societies—suggests that we are dealing with new forms of religion highly relevant to the modernization process.

These forms vary in membership from a handful of adherents to several million followers in a single movement. In black Africa there are thousands of individual movements; in Melanesia, the Philippines, Korea, Indonesia, and Brazil they are numbered in the hundreds; and there are lesser numbers in the rest of the Americas, the Caribbean countries, Polynesia, tribal India, and Southeast Asia—in fact wherever societies have been predominantly tribal or primal in nature. Perhaps some twenty million or more people are actually involved at any one time and spread across all continents.

Negative Attitudes and Dysfunctional Aspects

The common reaction to these movements, if they are recognized at all, is to regard them as simply irrelevant or else as reactionary obstacles to real development. This negative attitude may be encouraged by some of the more lurid, tragic, or irrational events or the unbalanced or misunderstood leaders who do emerge from these new religious movements and who secure great publicity at the time. Thus, in 1964, the world's press carried headlines concerning the tragic encounter between Alice Lenshina's independent Lumpa church and the first African government of Zambia, under Kenneth Kaunda, and this conflict now provides a debating issue for scholars.[4] An earlier clash involved Joseph Chilembwe and the first independent church in Malawi in the ill-fated but now famous Shire Rising against the colonial government in 1915, and this also has an extensive and growing literature.[5] Many other less dramatic examples could be mentioned, especially of clashes between governments and these new prophets, although closer examination will often show that the government has been misinformed and has acted unjustly.[6]

It is therefore inevitable that there are two sides to the story we are to present here and briefer mention may first be made of where these independent religious movements serve to hinder development. For example, the magical worldview remains when new rituals are viewed as powers in themselves. The movements that totally reject Western medicine or modern education are harming at least some of their members. In the Ivory Coast a member of the new Kokamba movement was able to buy a powered bicycle with the money saved from expenditure on fetishes and sacrifices, but the same movement forbade the cultivation of nutritious yams and replaced them with cassava, thus aggravating the problem of malnutrition. Neither excessive discipline of prolonged fasting nor all-night rituals and exhausting ecstatic experiences produce people fit for work. The prophet's warnings against normal actions or journeys, such as "never travel on Tuesdays," interfere with rational economic activity. Likewise encapsulation within the comprehensive activities of an apolitical religious movement deprives credit unions, trade unions, and political structures of the support they need. New forms of conspicuous consumption can appear—in cathedralesque buildings, laces and frills, silks and satins in the prayer gowns, elaborate printing, rich vestments and high-status lifestyle for the leader, even if this is vicariously enjoyed with pride by his simple-living members.

Belief in having enlisted the "power of the Spirit" on one's behalf may lead to unrealistic attitudes toward one's own capacities and plans. On the other hand, the more millennial movements are escapist as far as the hard work of development is concerned; but even here the dreamed-of Utopia usually contains the goods or benefits brought by Western civilization and therefore implies acceptance of new needs, a criticism of the old order that failed to supply them, and a first attempt, albeit unrealistic, at a more modern reconstructed order. But in spite of these and other dysfunctional aspects, subtle changes in worldview are still occurring throughout most of these movements, and we are satisfied that the overall effect is on the credit side of the development ledger, as we must now seek to explain.

A current Zambian example: the Masowe Apostles

As an example of how these religious movements have been ignored or misunderstood by local, government, and international agencies, we take Marrapodi compound, a periurban squatter community to the north of Lusaka, the capital of Zambia. By the 1970s Marrapodi had grown to about 10,000 inhabitants and contained several indigenous religious groups or independent churches; the most striking of these were the apostles of John Masowe, the "Basketmakers' church." In 1965 the new Zambian government developed the Marrapodi Site and Service Scheme as the first systematic plan to upgrade an unauthorized settlement, both as pilot plan and showpiece.

The Masowe apostles have received their nickname, the "Basketmakers," for the excellence of the products of one of the numerous cottage industries they had been developing since the 1940s; these included metalworking, furniture making, charcoal manufacture, basketweaving, embroidery, machine sewing, crocheting, and food preparation, together with taxi and truck businesses; and where appropriate they used machine tools such as lathes, drills, and saws and electric generators. In the mid-1970s they were planning a trade-training center of their own. Many had built modern homes in Marrapodi and owned a car. At the same time they formed a fairly close community, organized in a highly communal manner. Together with other similar new religious groups, they gave an unusual cohesion to the life of Marrapodi, a discipline, an order, and a substantial economic activity that amounted to self-support for many of the inhabitants—features usually lacking in squatter communities.

The planning authorities seem to have taken almost no account of their development potential. Indeed, in 1973 in the course of some troubles between the Basketmakers and the government, they were warned against "creating their own empires" and not "integrating with the rest of the masses," and in Twapia, another township in the Copperbelt, in 1964 five hundred of the apostles had been allowed to remain only if they scattered all over the settlement. The self-help plan, especially for providing better housing, that was basic in the Marrapodi Site and Service Scheme, ignored the communal forms of self-help already so strikingly in evidence in the religious communities; neither these communities nor the cottage industries that had mushroomed with their support were acknowledged or explicitly considered a major factor in the development scheme—in effect, they were regarded as nonexistent or expendable, and they were not used as precious sources for motivation and control in community development.[7]

An earlier West African Example: The Harris Movement

The largest mass movement toward Christianity in West Africa derived from the peripatetic preaching of William Wade Harris, a Grebo from Liberia, who evoked an astonishing response among the coastal peoples of the Ivory Coast and western Ghana in the years 1913–15. Some 120,000 people are estimated to have abandoned magic objects and traditional rituals, accepted baptism from Harris, adopted the Sabbath, and built little churches while waiting for the whites who Harris promised would come and teach the Bible. Much of Harris's teachings had direct economic implications. The observance of traditional rituals and taboos had meant that it was scarcely possible go get four consecutive days of labor, and there was constant conflict between religious requirements and economic necessities; Harris enjoined six days of steady labor followed by a day of rest, the Sabbath. Fetishes that exercised much irrational control over people's lives were to be destroyed, and so they were. Likewise, taboos on many animals useful for food, but regarded as totemic, were removed. Expensive funeral customs, which involved wrapping the corpse in valuable cloths given by friends and sprinkling gold dust between the layers were forbidden. Alcohol was to be taken only in moderation, tobacco was banned, cleanliness and education were extolled. The French colonial administrators had long been striving for such changes in order to secure an orderly basis for development, but with little result; Harris had effected a dramatic breakthrough, which they had to acknowledge and welcome in spite of their characteristic secularism. The movement, however, got out of hand in some ways, and the outbreak of World War I changed the colonial situation so that the French deported Harris back to Liberia in 1915. The ongoing effects of the movement were seen in a great influx into the mission churches when they arrived later, and in the wide range of independent churches that continue to this day within the Harris tradition. The largest independent derivative from this tradition is the Déima, or Dahima, religion; in the 1980s a high-level French development expert visited this community regularly. He became so impressed with their development potential and achievements that he correctly suggested it is the ongoing Harris influence that lies behind much of the development that has occurred in the relatively prosperous Ivory Coast, as compared with the rest of Africa.[8]

Wide-ranging Examples

There is clearly, therefore, considerable potential for economic development in new religious movements of this kind, and attitudes of opposition or of indifference may show a serious failure to understand and to use the movements concerned. This development potential could be traced in many different and unlikely parts of the world: in the peyote religion among North American Indians, the Rastafarians of Jamaica, the Mama Chi movement in Panama, the Israelitas in Peru, the Ratana and Ringatu movements in New Zealand, the Daku community in Fiji, the new religions of Korea, the Paliau movement and Christian Fellowship Church in Melanesia, and some of the new religious communities of the Philippines. The largest of these is the Iglesia ni Cristo, with at least several thousand members. In 1964 it bought a large piece of isolated and rugged land in Nueva Ecija. Under its discipline and with its motivation, but without outside technical or financial aid, it has conquered the wilderness and established a prosperous community enjoying irrigated fields, a park, vineyards, a school, and a health center, together with home industries and some land for each family's own use. This is pioneering land reform in a country where this remains a basic problem.[9]

In order to give depth to this chapter the remaining examples will be drawn from black Africa, where we find the largest number of these movements, and the continent most dramatically in need of development.

Cultural Foundations for Economic Change: A New Worldview

Before proceeding further to details of the African movements and their economic activities, we should give some indication of those basic changes in the cultures of traditional societies that seem to be demanded if economic development is to occur, changes that lead to adoption of a whole new worldview. These may conveniently be examined in terms of five transitions: (1) from a *cosmos* based on necessary internal relations to one revealing contingent relationships; (2) from dealing with *power* through magic and ritual to dependence on science and faith; (3) by the addition of history to myth, as a new category for dealing with *time;* (4) from a *society* that is closed, unitary, and sacral, to one that is open, pluralist, and secular; (5) by seeing *evil* as involving moral rather than ritual pollution, and as located internally in the individual as well as externally in evil forces.

A summary account of these basic changes may now be given.

From a Closed Unitary, Sacralized Cosmos to an Open, Desacralized System with Contingent Interrelations. In the current atmosphere of new respect for primal religions we hear much of the harmony between the earth, the plant and animal creation, man and the spirit world. It is not generally realized that this reflects a particular view of the cosmos as a closed and unitary system, to be regarded as sacral at all points, with nature, man, and the gods each playing their *necessary* parts in maintaining the harmonious functioning of the whole. The keyword here is *necessary,* and the main concern is conservation of the given structures in their fixed interrelationships, including those of the creator to the creation.

In the Semitic view of the cosmos that is embedded in Western science and capacity for development, the creator remains free and sovereign over the creation, not limited by the nature of any preexistent raw material, nor compelled to create or play any *necessary* and fixed part in the operation of the world of nature and of man. At all points the relation between the divine and mankind is *contingent* upon the free will of the former and the free responses of the latter. Both parties exercise this freedom within the basic structures and principles of their being, so that the presence of the contingent factor does not lead to chaos. Similarly, modern microphysics has shown that chance and order are both present in nature and are not incompatible.

The effect of this view of the cosmos is to desacralize the natural world (and social structures also), to remove all built-in spirit beings from it, and so to open it to scientific exploration and to development of its vast potential. Man is no longer at the mercy of the natural environment, where disasters are liable to interpretation as the will of the spirit world. Nature is no longer left in its chaotic or undeveloped state, but is now a gift to be developed, controlled, and enjoyed. In undertaking these tasks man is responsible as steward to a God who transcends nature and enters into contingent relations with it. This desacralization position therefore has nothing to do with irresponsible desecration or exploitation of nature, but retains the primal religions' reverence for nature on a new basis that establishes man's freedom over against his environment and therefore his responsibility to it.[10]

This desacralized view of nature has its main historical origin in the religion of ancient Israel, as expressed in the Hebrew Scriptures. African independent churches are usually very conscious of the Bible so widely available to them in local vernaculars; it is their main reference point, in however confused or limited a fashion. This means that they are increasingly absorbing its desacralized understanding of the world and entering into a worldview able to encourage and sustain development. For example, they are no longer tied to the ancestral land and its sacred powers and places; these movements are free to spread far and wide according to their own choices and ambitions, and some have become remarkably international. Their places of worship are church buildings, to be erected anywhere required, and not confined to the local sacred places given by tradition or determined by the spirits. There is a new element of contingency, openness, and responsibility, replacing the fixities and fatalities of the old cosmology, a change of attitude that is a necessary prerequisite for development.[11]

Access to Power through Science and Religious Faith instead of Magic and Religious Rituals. In peoples and primal religions there are two characteristic ways of controlling the powers both of nature and of the spirit world—through magic or through the appropriate religious ritual. The former seeks to manipulate power through occult knowledge or skills, or potent objects, and the latter relies on ceremonies, sacrifices, words of power, the skills of specialists in the sacred, or the spirit powers present at sacred places. Hunting, herding, and agriculture may be authentic religious acts, controlled by ritual and taboos. At times these exhibit a genuine conservation value and represent an attempt to live in harmony with the environment. Although the magical and the religious attitudes may be distinguished in principle, and also vary considerably in their incidence in different peoples, in practice they tend to coalesce and gravitate toward the magical.

We should not need to emphasize the fact that reliance upon the efficacy of magic or religious ritual as causal agents to control the environment is incompatible with realistic action toward development. Access to the powers of nature depends on expanding the limited empirical, practical knowledge and skills, which even primitive societies possess, by science and modern technology. This fact is not denied when we recognize that science alone is not enough, and that moral and social factors are also highly relevant. Similarly, access to the powers of the spirit world is not controlled by religious ritual with inherent efficacy, but occurs through personal relationships marked by prayer and faith. Both of these changes correlate with the above change from a cosmology governed by necessity to one providing for contingency, and with a desacralized view of nature.

The religious history of Israel reveals a running battle between magic, witchcraft, occultism, and ritualism on the one hand, and on the other a reliance on the one supreme God who is approached in faith by prayer and obedience. This same battle is now being fought out in many of the new religious movements, and there is often a striking and explicit rejection (as in public fetish burnings) of any reliance upon magic and of any fear of witchcraft or the power of enemies or evil spirits. This removes mental inhibitions restricting action, especially new forms of action and the ensuing progress that will arouse the jealousy of others and lead to reprisals by magic or occult means. It is this fear that has beset the potentially progressive individual in most undeveloped societies. Members of these independent movements are much less likely to be frustrated by these fears or to squander their resources on ineffective magical or ritual procedures or occult countermeasures, for they possess superior spiritual resources. Formerly, they believed in a range of spirits that inhabited or controlled all natural forces and objects and that had to be placated or satisfied by repeated and expensive sacrifices, or otherwise avoided; now these are either believed in no longer, or they have lost their central position and power. We have already detailed some of the effects of the Harris movement in the Ivory Coast at these same points of magic and ritual.

The religious emphasis in most African movements is upon prayer, faith, and the power of the Holy Spirit, supported by fasting, symbolic objects, and charismatic leaders. New rituals do develop, but they are not economically wasteful (e.g., holy water healings), and their efficacy is not so much inherent as associated with obedience and faith.

The switch away from magic and ritual means a new emphasis on the importance of hard work, which is given a religious value. This is seen in new judgments on indolence and in economic enterprises such as those noted in the Ivory Coast and Zambian examples given earlier in this chapter. It is widely remarked that employers in many African countries prefer "Zionists" (the general term in local use, not connected with Jewish Zionism) or other members of new movements as employees because of their motivation, sobriety, health, and honesty.

The Addition of History to Myth in Dealing with Time. In spite of all the flux and change in the history of African peoples, their societies may be described as essentially conservative, looking along the lines of lineage and genealogy into the mythical past and thus finding legitimization for the present. As for the future, although there might be great changes at one level through wars, conquests, fission, natural disasters, or migrations, at the deeper levels of worldviews and basic social forms and sanctions no changes were desired, much less deliberately planned and worked for. Security lay in conservation of the resources and norms of the past, in repelling anything that might destroy these, and not in working for a better, ampler future on a new model. Religion was concerned with the regular renewal of the vitalities of man and nature, but not with their radical extension or transformation.

Eschatology in primal religions is characteristically either absent, undeveloped, or clearly conservative, with any paradise understood as restoration of something lost in the past, as following the models of the culture heroes, and maintaining reciprocity with the ancestors. In effect, this means "more of the same" rather than any real innovation.

Into this repetitive, conservative society there came the view that life is tied neither to the past nor to the levels of the present, but can progress to a consummation in the future. This is the revolution in worldview represented in secular form by development schemes and in religious form not only by the explicit millennialisms, but also by the ordinary achievements of the older churches and of the independents, and by the varying emphasis on eschatology within their teachings. After surveying various forms of religious innovation in central Africa one recent study from a Marxian viewpoint comments that

> it is amazing to see how the same few trends in symbolic development dominate them all. . . .All struggle with the conception of time. The cyclical present implicit in the old super-structure (i.e. world view) . . . becomes obsolete . . . it gives way to a linear time perspective that emphasizes personal career and historical development, even to the extent of interpreting history as a process of salvation in the Christian sense. . . .In some . . . they explicitly strive towards the creation of a new and fundamentally different community. . . .[12]

These are characteristic features of the Semitic outlook introduced into black Africa through the impact of the Bible, missions, and Western civilization, which has these views of time and history woven into its fabric. The myth form is still needed to deal with the relations between men and the divine, and especially with the boundaries of time, but it neither dominates the dealing with history nor is confined to the images of the past—eschatology has a new freedom to deal with the future.

The independent movements, along with the older churches, are conspicuous bearers of this new sense of time and the historical future. Some of the former are explicitly millennial and await the cataclysmic events that will introduce the new order. Others are less specific in their eschatology, but are sustained amid the frustrations of their present lot and the confusions of the new Africa by their hopes of the divine blessings that await them. Most of these churches have known historical founders, and their religious call experiences and subsequent histories replace the myths of the culture heroes as normative reference points. In addition, the new festivals that develop have origins that are biblical and historical rather than cosmic or mythological.[13]

There is also great pride and confidence in their church, and in the power of their god to overcome present problems and to introduce both the church and its members to a new future. This future is expressed perhaps in the rather grandiose name of the church, or in its sense of mission to mankind and its ultimate recognition by the older churches in Africa and beyond. For example, one West African church of modest size officially calls itself "The Church of the Lord, Throughout the World" and has backed this claim by spreading into some five West African countries, by establishing branches in Britain and the United States, and by joining the World Council of Churches; it has opened a theological seminary, its leader travels in a Mercedes-Benz, and its leading layman is a millionaire. For a church that emerged "from the bush," as it were, less than fifty years ago, this is an impressive record of self-development and advance in the modern manner, which has been possible only by breaking from the old confining worldview and entering into the stream of historical development.

From the Closed, Unitary, Sacral Society to the Open, Plural, Secular Society. In most traditional societies in Africa, the tribe, its rulers, and institutions were set within a sacred cosmic order that formed part of the traditional worldview. The patterns and the sanctions for social organization usually derived from this cosmic order, with its associated mythology, and the leaders of the society were important channels through which cosmic spiritual forces operated for its welfare; sharp separation between religious and political institutions and activities was rare. Such a society may be called unitary and sacral, or "ontocratic."[14]

It is not surprising therefore, that the earliest forms of independent church and of nationalist political movement were frequently associated, as religion and politics had been in the past. Political bodies often clothed themselves in religious forms, using hymns, prayers, catechisms and extensive quotations from the Bible. If such association had continued there would have been a tendency to perpetuate an ontocratic society with a new national religion woven into the new political structure. In the event, however, the religious and the political manifestations of independence have tended to move apart; the former have issued in what are now called the new religious movements, and the latter have taken the Western forms of trade unions, political parties, and independent national governments.

Even though African independent movements have not provided new national or state religions, and in Zaire the Kimbanguist church explicitly turned against this possibility, the new political powers tend to revert to the sacral position and so to create a unitary society and a one-party state on the old ontocratic model, with the head of state sometimes assuming a pseudomessianic and sacral status. Some independent churches have sought to gain advantage for themselves by supporting these tendencies, but most of them are emphatic in distinguishing between church and state and in following a policy of rendering unto Caesar only the things that are Caesar's. In this they stand together with the older churches in the battles between church and state that will continue to develop in various parts of Africa. They have done this by undermining the traditional mystiques of chiefship and of ethnic group, establishing many coexistent, specialized voluntary societies to proceed independently on an increasingly secular basis. They represent, therefore, the new open society where there are live options in religion, even if in politics many countries still exhibit no-option or one-party systems. This development has been possible because they have been able to resacralize so much of the common life of their members within the context of the new religious community, with its own biblical mythology, charter, and sanctions.

In addition, traditional societies were usually closed in another sense—in terms of being confined to a particular ethnic group, language, and culture, and a specific set of ancestors. In contrast to such "particularist" societies, the new religious movements often transcend these limitations and exhibit a "universalistic" potential that extends to mankind as such. The inherited biological ancestors are replaced by a new set of ancestors who in a sense have been freely chosen when joining the new movement. Central among these is the founder, who may well not be of one's own clan or tribe, and in due course members will discover their further ancestry in the Christian missions and churches that brought the faith to Africa and provide links back to the People of God in the Scriptures, and therefore to Adam as the universal ancestor of mankind.[15] The significant ancestors now depend on spiritual adoption rather than social inheritance.

The independent churches, therefore, are helping to achieve in one life span the passage from a closed, sacral, and unitary society to a modern secular state and religiously plural society capable of reaching beyond the limitations of clan, tribe, and language toward new national entities and new international relationships. This new community is a quite new social structure, not deriving from the lineage system, the age or occupation groupings of its members, and in many areas offering unheard-of opportunities for leadership both by women and by the young. It is a radically different voluntary social form and so is part of the transformation from the old to the new, both in societies and in worldviews.

Evil Involves Moral Rather than Ritual Pollution and is Located Internally as Well as Externally. All human activities have to recognize the existence of evil, and cultures vary considerably in how they understand evil, where they locate or identify it, and how they deal with it. These variations have important consequences for developmental processes, which involve the removal of a wide range of evils such as ignorance, sickness, hunger, oppression, discrimination, injustice, anomie, poverty, and wide wealth differentials across the world.

In many primal religions misfortunes are traced to ritual pollution such as the breaking of taboos and the neglect of certain sacrifices or ritual duties. Although we recognize that ritual purifications or the renewed observance of rites may have profound inner meanings and may function in a thoroughly sacramental fashion, it remains true that in practice dealing with evils in these terms is superficial in relation to the changes needed for development.

Likewise, the regular location of the evil forces that prevent development as always external to the individual or the society concerned distracts attention from the necessary internal changes. When stagnation, failure, misfortunes, and disasters are so readily blamed on one's fate or on demons and evil spirits, witches and sorcerors, or superior magic employed by one's enemies, then individual and corporate initiative, effort and responsibility, are undermined. Without these, there can be no development. In other words, the location of evil, and responsibility for it, must be internalized to a large extent.

At the same time, the undoubted existence of external evil forces must be seen in a different manner, in terms of evil social, economic, and political structures and traditions that must also be attacked and changed. In addition, many religious communities will recognize the existence of a single external evil force, power, or person pervading human existence—a Satan or a demonic principle, which the religion concerned has its own means of conquering.

At this last point the new religious movements in Africa make a major contribution when they escape from fear of angered ancestors or a world of evil spirits and occult powers. Sometimes all such forces are coalesced into a single evil power or Satan, but in either form there is a widespread conviction that the God of the new faith provides total victory and release, a new freedom to act with the prospect of success.

Perhaps more important is the internalization of responsibility so that the individual starts to share in the blame for sickness, lack of prosperity, failure in exams, trouble with the police and other problems; instead of immediately identifying external scapegoats one takes a measure of responsibility for one's own fate and welfare. This process of "individualization" and "responsibilization" is to be seen in the work of Albert Atcho, a highly charismatic prophet-healer within the Harris churches of the Ivory Coast. Each sick or distressed person must seek the source of his or her troubles in him or herself rather than in evil spirits or in enemies employing sorcery; these troubles include not only the traditional forms of sickness, but also all the problems of people undergoing great social changes.[16] This development of a sense of individual responsibility frees people from old fatalisms and fears and helps to replace the collapsing traditional social structures upon which people depended in the past. This deep personal transformation of ideas of causation, of evil, and of the spiritual world opens the way for new forms of human existence and development. It is not the same as what is called "individualism" as against a sense of communal responsibility in analyses of Western societies. Rather, it is the discovery of individual selfhood and maturity within cultural contexts which suppressed individual freedom. The economic effects of these new attitudes have been noted in the entrepreneurial features of the case studies given earlier in this chapter and will appear at many points in what is to follow.

Personal Prerequisites for Economic Development

We turn now to several particular issues that illustrate developmental prerequisites at a less fundamental level: the matters of attitudes toward work, education, health, and morality.

New Attitudes toward Work. The records of developmental schemes contain many variations on the story of the introduction of better agricultural methods that succeeded in doubling the rice crop, so that the amount of work needed for survival and the area planted were henceforth halved, no other changes occurred, and the social problems attendant upon the advancement of one individual or one part of the community were avoided. It is not a matter of Third World peoples being lazy, for many of them work incredibly hard merely to exist; it is a matter of motivations and goals, and of social structures within which they can operate successfully. It involves a different conception of work, its effect, and its purpose.

We have already noted the teaching of prophet Harris concerning regular labor, and the industriousness of the Masowe apostles as a self-supporting community. People do tend to prosper when they join these groups, not only because of moral reform, health improvement, less wasteful spending practices, and regular habits built around the seven-day week program of their new community, but also because of belief that they now have access to the power of the Spirit made available through these churches, their founders, and practices and through the Bible. This encourages confidence, initiative, perseverance, adaptability to the changing modern situations, and freedom from distraction through political or other hysterias. In South Africa, where there is great mobility of labor and also much unemployment, the Zionists are known for helping traveling members, assisting in finding work, securing permits, piloting newcomers around, and in general acting as a mutual-help society.

The problems that arise from the conjunction of traditional African and modern development work practices is liable to appear most clearly where there have been many European employers of African labor, as in South Africa, Kenya, and Zimbabwe. It is not surprising, therefore, to find reports of these employers expressing preferences for workers who belong to the independent churches, as we have observed above. This is not evidence for the exploitability of independent church members, for the same work attitudes have tangible results in areas other than that of employment.

One of these is the capacity to plan and carry out communal projects involving economic activity of a modern nature, such as the building of very large and impressive self-designed churches at the headquarters of a movement. The first of these, apart from those of the more sophisticated new African movements in Lagos, was the notable brick building erected entirely by John Chilembwe's members between 1911–13 at his Providence Industrial Mission headquarters, Chiradzulu, in what was then Nyasaland. An equally impressive church was erected in 1956–58 at the Sione (i.e., Zion) village of the new Lumpa church in northern Zambia; by 1967 the Kimbanguists in Zaire had built their own huge place of worship, and Shembe's church has a similar building at Ekuphakameni near Durban. It is tragic that the first two of these were completely destroyed by government order at the conclusion of the conflicts already referred to; but our point is reinforced by the remarkable and elaborate brick church built once more at Chiradzulu (1928–33) by the Providence Industrial mission after it had been allowed to start again.

A second tangible result is to be seen in the "upward mobility" of many members of independent churches and the successful entrepreneurs to be found among them. In Zimbabwe, Zionists who began as migrant laborers may now be found as prosperous farmers; among the *aladura* (i.e., praying) churches of Nigeria there are many wealthy men—traders, property owners, and the occasional business tycoon. The same upward mobility among the several score of independent churches among the South African Cape Colored Community is to be seen in the "Docks Mission" that is now a "respectable" middle-class church, or the denomination presided over by a millionaire scrap dealer.

Education and Health. Since the independent churches embrace the masses more conspicuously than the older churches, they tend to arouse a common image of illiterate peasants, villagers, and urban squatters set over against the extensive educational activities of the missions and older churches. Although many of the independents envy the status and influence so gained, most of them would regard this major diversion of resources and expectations into educational systems as having seriously weakened the spiritual power of the sponsoring churches. The earlier prophet-healing independents, more Pentecostal in nature, often turned away from education to a reliance on the superior powers of the Spirit and were satisfied with the charismatic qualities of their leaders. This attitude, however, has never become general. The founders and leaders of the larger and longer established independent movements have often been well educated, or have sought further education, and some of these movements have a notable educational activity without losing their spiritual dynamic.[17]

The Chilembwe already mentioned was educated in America and by 1906 could report 906 pupils in seven schools, and there is still a large school at Chiradzulu. In Uganda the notable Reuben Spartas claimed twenty-three schools in 1936 for his African Greek Orthodox Church; the Christ Apostolic Church in Nigeria had an educational system with six grammar schools and a teacher training college by the 1960s; and in Zaire the Kimbanguist schools had some one-hundred-thousand pupils by 1970. Even a small, remote body such as the "Kingdom," a communal, adventist, and perfectionist group, began its new village in Ghana about 1967 with a two-teacher school. The more sophisticated Ntwalanist church, split off from the Kimbanguists in Zaire, offers an extended statement of its educational philosophy.[18] And it is notable during the last two decades that the independents have had a strong desire to improve the educational standards of their own leaders and have worked with missions and other churches in various ways for this purpose.

On the subject of health, it is probably true that there is more sickness, both physical and mental, in Africa today than ever before in its history. In this situation the independent churches, especially the prophet-healing type that has predominated in the last sixty years, offer a widespread, easily accessible, and often free healing service based largely on spiritual means—faith, prayer, fasting, the sacramental use of holy water or oil, and the support of the believing community. Although some traditional herbal remedies or elementary Western patent medicines may also be used, resort to traditional magical or ritual methods is usually banned. Although these new methods cannot deal with urgent needs for surgery, with leprosy, elephantiasis, and many other scourges, they do undoubtedly prove beneficial over a wide range of psychosomatic ailments and even with the barrenness of women; at the same time they avoid the frustrations and inadequacies of the Western-type services and the potential harm of some traditional treatments. There is also an increasing tendency to combine the independent spiritual treatment with the Western almost entirely physical treatment, and where this is done there is probably no better total medical service available anywhere in black Africa.[19]

A New Ethic with Ascetic Features. We shall concentrate here on one particular ethical issue that has the greatest importance for any developing area. It is generally acknowledged that the generation of internal capital, and high priorities for the basic substructures of economic and social development, have an overwhelming urgency in the development situation, and that what is known as "conspicuous consumption," an emphasis on luxury goods, is to be avoided. In moral terms this implies something akin to the Protestant work ethic, together with a certain simplicity in style of life.

African societies have always had their moral codes, but when we look for an ascetic component this does not seem to figure in African cultures. This becomes clearer when we compare the African image of the ideal or exemplary man with that to be found in many parts of Asia, especially in India. In the latter, although power and status may be admired or envied, it is the ascetic, the holy man or hermit, who represents the highest ideal; in mid-life the successful or professional businessman may abandon the world to follow the ascetic way. In the case of Gandhi, the ascetic life for himself and the simple life for all was the Indian way toward development.[20] By contrast the cultures of black Africa, despite elements of discipline or sacrifice associated with the training of some religious specialists and such remarkable role models as that of the Mugwe in Kenya, the dominant image is that of the successful man of vitality, power, prosperity, and wealth, which is measured in terms of wives, cattle, and lands. If he was a chief his people shared in this success, for he lived close to them and his resources were available to the community. Although there was little conspicuous consumption for the sake of prestige, the model contrasts with that which is so striking in Indian tradition.

In modern conditions the African model of modest but shared success has been inflated and distorted into that of the "Big Man" with a self-centered life-style encouraged by ready access to Western luxury goods—smart houses, status cars, expensive furniture, and flamboyant parties with imported drinks. The same model appears in many of the older churches, with flamboyant clothes, expensive weddings, imported pipe organs quite inappropriate to the local conditions, a desire for prestigious modern cathedrals or merely for a church tower higher than that in the next village. All this widens the serious gap between rich and poor and consumes the resources so badly needed for development. Western Christians, with their comparative affluence, cannot import the ascetic critiques they do have in their own traditions, and African cultures lack a sufficiently strong corrective.

It is among many of the independent churches that we find a radically different, simple life-style. Leaders often abandon the "Big Man" image for simplicity of manner, dress, and housing. The founder of the Brotherhood of the Cross and Star in Calabar walks rather than use the church car, dresses in shirt and trousers, and sits on the floor in church like an Indian ascetic. Around the turn of the century, Dr. Majola Agbebi of eastern Nigeria neither smoked nor drank, was a vegetarian, ate lightly, fasted often, and taught this style in his Native Baptist Church. The spiritual head of the great Kimbanguist church, Joseph Diangienda, dresses as simply as Nyerere; the elderly man, barefoot and in plain white prayer gown leading a preservice Bible class in the Celestial Church of Christ in Ibadan turned out to be the deputy vice-chancellor of the great University of Ibadan—and this in Yoruba country, where the conspicuous-consumption syndrome is visible everywhere. Right across Africa the independents are known by their plain prayer gowns, enlivened with colored sashes and marks of office, but still a simple, cheap, and noncompetitive community costume. Some large denominations even forbid church buildings as wasteful and unnecessary, but this is in drier climatic areas.

There is one aspect of the ethic of the independent movements that demands special attention. They almost all ban the use of alcohol and tobacco; here they part from the custom of using palm wine and cereal beer socially and ritually, and from the life-style of much of modern Africa.

The latter has been catered to and shaped by two of the earliest forms of industrialization in many African countries, the cigarette factory and the modern brewery. Cameroun government tourist literature boasts that brewing is the largest industry in the country and assures the visitor that canned or bottled beer will be available anywhere upcountry, even if other goods may be in scarce supply. These industries are capital instead of labor intensive, employ high rather than intermediate technology, and produce nothing but luxury consumer goods that do everything to increase rather than solve the health and social problems of the country. In other words, this form of industrialization is economic madness, as well as morally indefensible in a developing nation. The social cost of alcohol and tobacco in the economically advanced nations is increasingly under question; in black Africa it is intolerable. The sound social and moral instinct of the independent religious movements in these matters is quite remarkable, especially when we remember that the economic argument employed above is unknown to them, and that many have departed from the ethic of their parent churches or of the surrounding missions (e.g., Catholic, Lutheran, Anglican, Afrikaner, etc.) without anyone urging abstention upon them. Without attempting here to explain this aspect of their ethic we can safely assert that at this point the independents with their millions of members are making a substantial contribution, albeit unrecognized, to the social and economic development of Africa.

Specific Economic Activities

The industrial, agricultural and marketing activities of these religious movements demonstrate that the new worldviews, work ethics, and other changes do have tangible economic results. Sometimes they focus on agricultural development, as with the plantations at Agege of the "African" churches in Lagos around the turn of the century, and those of the Providence Industrial Mission about the same time, or the more recent agricultural settlements of the Kimbanguist church, which in 1969 had 313 settlers at Lutendale and was run like a kibbutz, with young offenders and unemployed youths sent there for training while developing the oil-palm, banana, and manioc plantations; the cattle, chicken and fish farms. On the industrial side, the same church has had furniture, tailoring, and motor repair workshops, as well as various social and health services. The Apostolic Revelation Society of Ghana, under prophet Wovenu, has attempted petrol filling stations, chicken farms, animal husbandry, a *kente* clothmaking cooperative, and other enterprises; his "holy city" headquarters at Tadzewu is an example of modern town planning, but African in style, and there are many other examples of such "new Jerusalems."

The most famous and distinctive of these is Aiyetoro ("happy city"), of the Holy Apostles' Community, amid the mangrove lagoons east of Lagos. This should be closely studied by anyone concerned with African development. Founded in this remote area in 1947 by a group of dissident "Cherubim and Seraphim," they changed their name, within a year adopted a radically communal order of life, even breaking up the family system, and then under a strong central and religious control began economic development and industrialization that led to their description in 1951 as "the most successful community development in Nigeria"; and all this without external model, stimulus, or assistance, and without becoming Westernized. By the 1970s the Utopian communalism had been replaced by a mixed economy with some degree of private enterprise and with some social stratification replacing the earlier egalitarianism, and yet without destroying the community; indeed other adjacent communities had been taken into the system. The short history of Aiyetoro provides a fascinating study of the interplay of social, economic and religious forces in one of these new religious movements, with obvious relevance to the Weber-Tawney theses and to African development in general.[21]

Even if Aiyetoro should collapse, and even though some of the Wovenu, Kimbanguist, and other enterprises above did fail, the record of the independent movements shows considerable potential, much hard achievement, and a determined intention to share in the economic and social development of Africa. New economic units, rationally developed for economic purposes and where necessary able to transcend ethnic and even national divisions, have appeared within the context of the new movements; these have provided important channels whereby new ideas and techniques flow into the more rural areas, and they encourage people to plan, organize, and learn the difficult art of handling money, all set within the incentives and the disciplines that a religious body can provide.

Conclusion

The special significance of these new religious movements lies in their influence and efforts being spontaneous and locally generated, indigenous in rationale, method, and form, and in the kind of new order that is envisaged; to this extent they are nearer the grass roots of local life and less Westernized.

They represent a noninstrumental view of the relationship between religion and development. In this sense, to ask whether these new religious movements are a help or hindrance to development implies too external a view of the relationship; rather one should ask if the kind of development we have surveyed is integral to these movements' own existence, with roots in both the indigenous and the biblical worlds. This has been well put for the Basketmakers' church in Zambia in a way that can also sum up the burden of this essay:

> The traditional and the modern, the old and the new, continue to merge; and it is perhaps the greatest strength of the Apostles that they manage to cope with both in a manner which is both suited to, and in accordance with, the capacity of their followers to absorb. The result, however, is not merely a syncretistic blend of traditional and the modern but rather the creation of a new African response to social change within a meaningful context."[22]

Here, in the new religious movements in primal societies, there lies a largely unrecognized but nevertheless ongoing and substantial religious contribution to the problem of a world starkly divided into rich and poor nations.[23]

NOTES

1. The opening section of this essay owes much to an address at the Selly Oak Colleges in April 1983 by professional development economist Dr. Charles Elliott, now director of Christian Aid; this was published in May 1983 as *Pains*

of 'Ungrowth' by the Catholic Missionary Education Centre, London. Some of the material on Africa in the following notes appeared in *World Development* 8 (1980): 523–33, under the title "African Independent Churches and Economic Development."

2. Notable exceptions are the Anglican bishops under Idi Amin, Desmond Tutu, and others in South Africa, and works such as F. O. Segun's *Cry Justice* (1967) and H. Okullu's *Church and Politics* (1974).
3. For a world survey see H. W. Turner, "Tribal Religious Movements," *Encyclopedia Britannica* (1974 edition), *Macropaedia* 18: 697–705.
4. For a sympathetic and also Marxist-oriented major survey, see W. M. J. van Binsbergen, "Religious Innovation and Political Conflict in Zambia . . . the Lumpa Rising," *African Perspectives,* no. 2 (1976): 101–35.
5. The foundation work is G. Shepperson and T. Price, *Independent African: John Chilembwe and the . . . Native Rising of 1915* (Edinburgh: Edinburgh University Press, 1958).
6. See further, H. W. Turner, "Prophets and Politics: A Nigerian Test-case." *Bulletin, Society for African Church History* 2, no. 1 (December 1965): 97–118; repr. in H. W. Turner, *Religious Innovation in Africa* (Boston: G. K. Hall & Co., 1979), 133–45.
7. See Bennetta Jules-Rosette, "Marrapodi: An Independent Religious Community in Transition," *African Studies Review* 18 no. 2 (1975): 1–16; also C. M. Dillon-Malone, *The Korsten Basketmakers: A Study of the Masowe Apostles* (Manchester: Manchester University Press, 1978).
8. The most accessible historical source is G. M. Haliburton, *The Prophet Harris* (Harlow: Longman Group, 1971); a specific study is S. S. Walker, "Religion and Modernization in an African Context: The Harris Church of the Ivory Coast," *Journal of African Studies* 4, no. 1 (1977): 77–85.
9. See R. L. Deats, "Iglesia ni Cristo," *Church and Community* (Manila), (September-October 1967): 26–28; the main study is A. L. Tuggy, *Iglesia ni Cristo* (Quezon City: Conservative Baptist Publishing Inc., 1976).
10. See P. Gheddo, *Why Is the Third World Poor?* (Maryknoll, NY: Orbis Books, 1973).
11. See W. M. J. van Binsbergen "Religious Innovation," *African Perspectives* (1976a), 111–16; also his "The Dynamics of Religious Change in Western Zambia," *Ufahamu* 6, no. 3 (1976), especially pp. 72, 75, 78. For a fuller account, see his *Religious Change in Zambia. Exploratory Studies* (London: Kegan Paul International, 1981), especially 154–66; also 266–316 on the Lumpa Rising.
12. W. M. J. van Binsbergen, "Religious Innovation," African Perspectives (1976a), pp. 111–12.
13. See extended example in M. L. Daneel, *Old and New in Southern Shona Independent Churches:* vol. 2, *Church Growth* (The Hague: Mouton & Co., 1974), 325–36.
14. See H. W. Turner, "The Place of Independent Religious Movements in the

Modernization of Africa," *Journal of Religion in Africa* 2, no. 1 (1969): 49–56; repr. in H. W. Turner, *Religious Innovation in Africa* (1979), 302–8.

15. Some new movements identify with the Israelites or the Jews in the Bible and call themselves the People of Judah (in Uganda), the Israelites (South Africa), or God's Kingdom Society (Nigeria). This represents the same process.
16. See M. Augé *et al., Prophétisme et Thérapeutique: Albert Atcho* (Paris: Hermann, 1975), especially chap. 4.
17. Fuller treatment in H. W. Turner, "African Independent Churches and Education," *Journal of Modern African Studies* 13, no. 2 (1975): 295–308.
18. See G. Mwene-Batende, "Le phénomène de dissidence des sectes religieuses d'inspiration kimbanguiste," *Cahiers du Cedaf,* 6 (1971), série 4: *Religion,* 28–37.
19. For a detailed study of healing in one West African independent church, see H. W. Turner, *African Independent Church* (Oxford: Clarendon Press, 1967), vol. 2, chap. 13.
20. See L. and S. Rudolf, *The Modernity of Tradition* (Chicago: Chicago University Press, 1967), especially 192–239.
21. See a number of works by S. R. Barrett: "Crisis and Change in a West African Utopia," in E. B. Harvey, ed., *Perspectives on Modernization* (Toronto: University of Toronto Press, 1972), 160–81; *Two Villages on Stilts* (New York and London: Chandler Publishing Company, 1974); *The Rise and Fall of an African Utopia* (Waterloo: Wilfrid Laurier University Press, 1977). These works do not claim to deal with the religious dimension in any depth.
22. C. M. Dillon-Malone, *The Korsten Basketmakers,* 130.
23. For a profound discussion of some of the basic issues, but without reference to new religious movements, see a seminal essay by the Indian scholar M. M. Thomas, "Modernization of Traditional Societies and the Struggle for New Culture Ethos," in J. Matthes, ed., *International Jahrbuch für Religions-Soziologie* (Koln: West Deutscher Verlag, 1970) 6: 45–64.

7

The Mission of the Churches Amid the Social Reality of Rich and Poor Nations

PAUL BOUVIER

Introduction

It doesn't take any special insight to understand that there is a relationship between social reality and the problem of God. Modern atheism—as in the past—has been taking much of its substance from the social conditions in which people live today. When Karl Marx proclaimed that "religion is the opium of the people," he was considering the situation of the working classes in nineteenth-century England. He felt that the main point was not "to explain the world, but to change it." Similarly, the French philosopher Jean-Paul Sartre stated: "the poor are hungry, and they are offered a crucifix."

The impact of social reality upon the religious sphere, faith, the churches, and God is even greater today, since, to quote Pope Paul VI in his encyclical on development, "social problems and social reality have reached the world level."[1] This increased awareness of social reality and its dramatic aspects does not only pertain to individual misery, still very much present in most of the world; by its global and structural aspects, this has become a matter of the world as a whole. Additionally, since the mass media and communication systems have more or less connected all people as if they were the members of a large family, interactions quite naturally developed among them, affecting their ideologies and their ways of thinking.

In primitive societies, at a time when science and technology were not developed to the same extent as today, religious faith could somehow manage to coexist with the determinisms of nature, which often coincided with the religious perspective. But the general evolution of the world, along with the progress of science, caused mankind to change its mentality. The feeling emerged that it was possible to influence nature as an object, to change living conditions, and, as Descartes stated it, man began to hope to "become master and owner of nature," to subdue it—all of this without any reference to God.

Emergence of a New Spirit

This emergence of a new, secular view of things was bound to have an impact on the exploitation of the world and its resources. The world, separated from its creator and origin, became a mere object that could be taken over and made use of, including humans and material goods.

As a matter of course, Christendom has also known plundering, violence, and contempt of human life in earlier times. Humans have always been possessed by the *libido dominandi et possedendi*. But it seems that with the awareness of new opportunities man's desire for profit even increased to the point of becoming the supreme rule.

Thus, the Western world became the focal point of scientific progress and development in technology. Europe broke out of its boundaries; its navigators, adventurers, scholars, technicians, and even its missionaries went into the world. Raw materials—metals, spices, and textiles—arrived in Europe. People got used to this supply of goods and wanted to secure it. This was the beginning of the colonies.

Colonization and Decolonization

This is not the proper place to recall the history of colonization and its often dramatic situations. The discovery of new countries, frequently followed by their conquest, may have resulted in some occasional benefits to them, but more often than not the exploitation of the colonies reduced them to the state of second-class nations whose resources were plundered and whose cultures were annihilated. What is left of this today?

With the decolonization starting after World War II, a new contact was established between the richest countries and the so-called developing, or poorest, countries. The gap between these two groups of nations is ever increasing, and so is the economic dependence. The resulting tensions are creating an imbalance and a conflict situation that may, in the long run, jeopardize world peace. A substantial assistance to these lesser developed countries is only conceivable if there is a deep modification of existing trade patterns.

What role can religions and the churches fulfill in that area, and what can they who proclaim a God of goodness and justice do in addition to international efforts, in order to remedy this great problem confronting believers and all mankind?

Technical Problems and the Churches

Jean-Jacques Rousseau accused Christians of being absent from the world's problems, arguing that "the Christian's home is not of this world."[2] It would indeed be a tragedy if believers and religions were unable to deal with a situation where "the hungry people challenge those living in opulence."[3]

First of all, it should be said that, because of their very nature, religions and Christian churches have no special, technical competence in bringing solutions to social problems. Above all, the church is "the proclamation and the transmission of a message of peace."[4] Neither are the churches to take the place of governments and statesmen in elaborating programs and making plans; but they can contribute more than programs and plans in reminding man of his dignity as "son of God" and the necessity of practicing love. "As you did it to one of the least of these my brethren, you did it to me."[5]

Social Problems Have Reached the World Level

Confronted with the gap between rich and poor nations, Pope Paul VI found the correct approach: "Social problems have reached the world level . . . the hungry people dramatically challenge those living in opulence. The Church invites everyone to respond with love to the call of their brother."[6] Pope Leo XIII already confronted the "undeserved misery of the poor" in his encyclical *Rerum Novarum;*[7] today, the poor are no longer just individuals, but entire nations that become increasingly poor, while other nations become increasingly rich.

Though all nations have been affected to some degree by the present crisis, it can be said that today's proletariat consists of entire nations of victims of economic difficulties and the mechanisms of trade, carrying the burden of foreign debts and unable to overcome their lack of technological development.

On this matter, the World Council of Churches, as well as

representatives from other religious communities, have expressed the same feelings of anguish as Pope Paul VI.

Faith Leads to Action

When Christian and other churches discuss the problems of this world, they do it out of their faith, which commands them to get involved in it. "But it is this religious mission itself that gives the function, the insight and the power which can constitute and strengthen the community of men according to divine law."[8] In other words, when the human values of justice and brotherhood, the concepts of well-being and prosperity, are integrated into the framework of religion or Christianity, they receive new depth and strength they would otherwise be lacking.

For instance, poverty becomes a sacred thing in God's sight, since it is like the shadow of the one who became poor for our sake, so that we might become rich (2 Cor. 8:9). We also know how much the "poor of Jahveh," the "Anawim" were cherished by God. The rights of the poor were protected: "You shall not oppress a hired servant who is poor and needy. . . . "(Deut. 24:14). The same was true for the widow and the orphan.

Justice in the Thought of the Fathers of the Church

Similarly, when speaking of "justice," the prophets meant the right of every member of the community to take part in common resources. This vision of sharing in the community had a tremendous impact on the Fathers of the church, the theologians of the third and fourth century C.E. (Saint Basil, Saint John Chrysostom, Saint Ambrose) and on the theologians of the Middle Ages as well (Saint Thomas Aquinas). In Ambrose's own words: "What you give to the poor you do not take from your own property; rather, you give back to him what is already his. It is common property, given for the use of all, which you claim for yourself. The earth was given to all, not only to the rich."[9] Saint Basil adds: "You commit as many injustices as there are people to whom you could give."

The values of justice and charity (love) have a dimension when they appear in a climate of religious faith, and they can go beyond the horizons of the merely legal, social, and economic viewpoints. In his *Pensées,* Blaise Pascal commented: "Man goes infinitely beyond man." Thus, religions definitely do have a role to play in the search for solutions to the problems of the poor nations of the world.

Initiatives within the Catholic Church and Elsewhere

On the practical level, as far as the Catholic church is concerned, we should remember the proposal made by Paul VI in Bombay, in 1964, to create a "world fund" taken from the military expenses of the nations and destined to solve the problems of the underprivileged (food, clothing, shelter, and medical care). We can find the same meaning in the creation of "Justice and Peace," an organism of the universal church through which the Catholic community is to promote the development of the poorer areas of the world and social justice among the nations.

This is not to mention the participation of the various Christian and non-Christian churches in the activities of international organizations dealing with social, economic, and humanitarian questions: the U.N. High Commissioner for Refugees, the Economic and Social Council, the Human Rights Commission, the International Labor Office, the World Health Organization, UNICEF, UNCTAD, the Red Cross, etc.

These activities are a strong argument in favor of cooperation between the churches and the international organizations in order to bring help and relief to those individuals and nations who need it most.

The church quite naturally became interested in helping poor countries. As we have just seen, the churches naturally felt that to live in communion with God meant to contribute, as much as possible, to the coming of justice. This is true for the World Council of Churches, for the various reformed congregations, and for other religious communities.

The Building of a Community of Life

As we have explained above, the mission of the churches consists first of all in conveying a message of peace and love to the people; but it should be added that it is also the mission of the church to build a community of life.

Though it is not a model for the secular society, it is a leaven of social life . . . there is a correlation between the life and dynamism within the Church and its commitment to serve mankind. There is a correspondence between the practice of faith and Christian life within the Church and the establishment of civilization of peace and brotherhood of men. . . Community life within the Church is a school of humanism (universal character of love between human beings, respect of man as an image of God and brother of Christ, need of a personal and collective conversion, finality of life giving its meaning to history and to the development of mankind).[10]

Sharing and Deaconship

The necessity of sharing in the church—namely in the Catholic church—is beautifully symbolized by the sharing of the Eucharist. There "the gift of God and the gift of life . . . the Easter resurrection and the liberation of man . . . are blended into one . . . as well as the obligation for the Church to feel daily solidarity towards the poor and the oppressed, to consider the act of sharing as sacred."[11]

And thus we can say that the mission of the church is "diacony," or service to the others, "actualizing the love of the neighbor," as a sign of the belonging to Christ.

In Christian history, the Christian's love has been the leaven of life in the church of the Middle Ages. "Being often the bulwark of the weak against the strong, the defender of the widow and the orphan, the Church constantly sought to humanize wars and to prevent them, to take care of the prisoners and the wounded and, in a more general way, to serve people in the fields of health, educations and development."[12]

Caritas Internationalis

Nowadays, this involvement of the church appears in a slightly different way in the shape of Caritas Internationalis. This organization, together with other nongovernmental organizations (NGO's) contributes to the humanitarian action of the church toward populations that are victims of war or otherwise affected by disasters and to the organization of aid to refugees and prisoners of war.

Caritas was first created for urgent help in case of disaster; but it soon had to go beyond this step of emergency assistance in order to work for the development of the countries in which it was active.

With the collaboration of other agencies, Caritas Internationalis is implementing aid programs in several countries where the population is oppressed by poverty.

Through its branches in 120 nations, Caritas is thus doing its part to fill the gap between those who have much—sometimes too much—and those who are in want of the most basic commodities.

Specific Programs

The following examples of activities undertaken by Caritas-Switzerland (a branch of Caritas Internationalis) can serve as an illustration.

In Mali, in the Sahel, farmers are leaving their villages to escape the drought. Since 1972, Caritas has been involved in creating deep enough water holes and dams for irrigation to enable people to stay in their villages.

On December 13, 1982, an earthquake devastated numerous towns and villages of Yemen. After some emergency relief operations, Caritas helped rebuild destroyed water containers.

In Bangladesh, poorest of the poor among the nations, Caritas produces a small pump in its mechanics workshop. This hand pump, suited for irrigating fields, allows small farmers to grow crops during the dry season, which is the only way to survive when the monsoon has not been good.

Chad has been at war for many years. Everything is disorganized, and in the dioceses of Sarh, Pala, N'Djamena, and Moundou only the church is able to maintain a minimum subsistence level: schools, sanitary equipment, emergency food supplies, etc. Along with other organizations, Caritas has been providing these dioceses with the necessary financial means.

Economics of Giving

Speaking of the churches in general, we could call for a crusade of all people of faith, aiming at manifesting the love of the worshippers of a same God. This should be done in the name of generosity. In his book *L'economie du XXeme Siecle* (Twentieth-century Economics),[13] the well-known economist Francis Perroux mentions what he calls the "economics of giving (giving—its economic significance in today's capitalism)," implying the need to have charity and solidarity become significant elements in the mechanisms of economics. In the encyclical *Mater et Magistra* Pope John XXIII said: "Justice and humanity request that the rich nations offer their help to those who need it. To divert, or even to waste goods necessary for the life of human beings is a sin against justice."[14] Finally, let us quote Vatican II: "Laymen should gladly offer their socio-economic contribution to the developing peoples; this cooperation is particularly commendable when it aims at establishing institutions affecting the fundamental structures of social life or intended for the education of those bearing the responsibility for public life."[15]

The Churches as a Motivating Force

As we have said so far, the role of the churches is not essentially to organize assistance programs between rich and poor nations. This is the task of men of heart who realize what a tragedy could result from the existing imbalance if it remains unchanged. The churches should contribute their moral and material help to this common task.

But the main task of the church is, actually, to do everything possible in order to convince people of the urgency of this question so that they may, willingly or reluctantly, undertake the necessary efforts to avert a major catastrophe on the international level.

This is not only a matter pertaining to the international order. Faith, belief, and religious life are equally at stake. As a matter of fact, it is impossible to speak of a God of love and a divine providence in the midst of chaos and hatred.

John Paul II and Human Rights

Therefore, and as a conclusion, we would like to mention the efforts made by Pope John Paul II on the international level, efforts reflecting both courage and love. "The opinions expressed by the Pope, as a spiritual leader with considerable moral authority, can contribute, to a certain extent, to raising the consciences of the people on the national and international level. . . . His stand on the matter of human dignity, and particularly his protest against repeated violations of the most fundamental rights are likely to be heard . . . namely in countries with a Catholic majority, in some of which grave violations are being committed today. . . Given the absence of appropriate international procedures, the Pope is in a position, by speaking out, among others, to convey a considerable moral power to the cause of human rights, under the pressure of public opinion."[16]

NOTES

1. Paul VI, *Populorum Progressio,*1967.
2. Jean-Jacques Rousseau, *Du Contrat Social,* IV, VIII.
3. Paul VI, 3.
4. Vatican II, *Gaudium et Spes,* 8–9.
5. Matthew 25:40.
6. Paul VI, 3.
7. *Rerum Novarum,* 1891.
8. Vatican II, *Gaudium et Spes,* 42.
9. Quoted from Pelanque, *Saint Ambroise et l'Empire Romain*(Paris: de Boccard, 1933), 366ff.
10. *Manuel de Secours en cas de catastrophe* (Rome: Caritas Internationalis 1983).
11. Ibid., 19.
12. Ibid., 20.
13. Francis Perroux, *L'Economie du XXeme Siecle* (Paris: P.U.F., 1961).
14. John XXIII, *Mater et Magistra,* 1962.
15. Vatican II, *ad gentes,* 41.
16. *Jean-Paul II et lest Droits de l'Homme* (Fribourg, Switzerland: Editions Universitaires, 1980).

8

God is Parent: Rich and Poor Nations are Siblings

GORDON L. ANDERSON

Introduction

In the Unification Church, God is viewed as the parent of the world with all people as God's children. When we talk about rich and poor nations in relationship to theology, this concept becomes a central factor. Any discussion of the relationship between rich and poor nations necessarily involves the belief that people of all nations are siblings. The sibling metaphor denotes a relationship that goes beyond economic or military considerations.

However, in the past, the concept of God as father of the world has often supported paternalism. As a result, many theologians today are hesitant to use it. I want to argue that there is a validity to the concept of God as parent, and its abuse does not destroy the central truth behind it.

Problems with God as Parent

The idea of God as father of the world is a Christian concept. In the New Testament, Jesus Christ called God his father; and, so has it been with many Christians to follow. Today however, the notion of God as father had been seriously challenged by many feminist and liberation theologians. For example, Mary Daly has written a book titled *Beyond God the Father* in which she proclaims "the death of God the Father" and the end of "phallic morality" derived from it.[1] Similarly, Joseph Comblin of Chile has written critically of the domination that is often associated with the image of God as father:

> Countless poor people are obsessed by the image of a false god with which other threaten them. They must be freed from this obsession. There is a certain monotheistic god who serves as the foundation and support of all kinds of domination: that of the father, the teacher, the master, the owner, the state, and the army. This god is a god of power,

and he sacralizes all power. He is the god of the ego, . . . the image and justification of every kind of individualism. In an individualistic society this god finds it easy to move around . . . We are not to give the name or title of "father" to any human being.[2]

These theologians are primarily reacting against authority that has been used to oppress and exploit people. The father figure, for them, is associated with the paternalistic economic and political control held by many Westerners. But to protest against corrupt paternal authority figures is not new. In Western history, for example, we have the Lutheran rebellion against the papacy and the political revolutions against the French and English monarchies. Today, when we mention the idea of someone proclaiming himself to be "father" of a society, we are inevitably reminded of Adolf Hitler, Jim Jones, or some other leader who has claimed fatherhood but appeared to embody evil. The reaction to fatherhood is a reaction to coercive power in general.

There is a problem if this reaction is taken too far, if all authority structures and traditions are rejected. For example, the papacy is sometimes believed to embody the same "satanic" fatherhood as psychopathic tyrants. The Enlightenment in the eighteenth century threw its intellectual weight against the church. But there is something to be said for the authority of tradition and parents. It is as presumptuous to think that the existing generation can create its own civilization as it is to think a baby can grow to maturity without parental guidance. Certainly our own insights and discoveries should assist in making decisions; however, our habits and cultural conditioning inform the intuitive aspect of our decision making, and we rely heavily upon this facility for survival.

God, as parent, implies that something comes before us, creates us. God, as parent, implies purpose for humans in a cosmos greater than humanity. God, as parent, implies an authority that comes before us whose rejection is foolishness; it is an authority that checks the pretensions of ultimacy in any individual person or nation, or humanity as a whole. Theologian Karl Barth viewed rejection of all supernatural authority as an arrogant attempt for humanity to create its own world, apart from its original purpose. Criticism of unjust authority is appropriate; however, rejection of authority per se is throwing out the baby with the bathwater.

Modern science, especially social science, has adopted a worldview that assists the emotional rejection of authority with its intellectual rejection. Sociologist Edward Shils has criticized his peers as follows:

> The traditionality which was pervasive in the *ancien regime,* but not to the exclusion of interest and power, helped to sustain these other features of society which were abhorrent to rationalists, secularists, progressives, and egalitarians. Traditionality became associated with a particular kind of society and culture . . . The first entry on the agenda of the Enlightenment was to do away with traditionality as such; . . .
>
> Tradition enters into the constitution of meaningful conduct by defining its ends and standards and even its means . . . Located at the boundaries of deliberate actions, setting the end or the rules and standards—the traditional stands around the boundaries of the field in which deliberate expediential actions and those filled with passion occur. Traditions here are often the "tacit component" of rational, moral, and cognitive actions, and of affect, too.[3]

Shils further noted that science itself has formed a tradition, as have revolutionary movements. Yet these traditions are heavily informed by their immediate past, even though they were consciously seeking to escape that past. Biology also teaches that the present is dependent upon the past, for life and environment. Children are dependent upon parents; this is the nature of the human life cycle. God as parent can symbolize the creative origin and influx of the necessary elements of human existence; the "tacit component" of our good actions transmitted subconsciously through tradition and the biosphere that nourishes human bodies. From this viewpoint, God as parent cannot be eliminated from interaction with human beings, even if they cognitively deny this is taking place. One cannot escape this type of dependence in life, even though one works for liberation from coercive and exploitive authority.

When the Unification Church describes God as parent, it must be prepared to address the current worldwide negative reaction to God the Father. Indeed, Unification theology readily acknowledges that the evils perpetrated by the perverse examples of fatherhood mentioned above are worthy of criticism as "satanic fatherhood."[4] However, whereas many Western theologians want to make God so abstract as to transcend human predicates like father, and thus the criticisms associated with these predicates, Unificationists want to preserve the concept of God as parent. Therefore, a different understanding of God as parent, one that transcends the current criticisms of God the Father but addresses our dependence on the creative past, is necessary. Unification theology describes God, the creator, as a parent.[5]

Problems with God as Love

Besides viewing God as our creative past and our ground of being, Unification theology also sees God as directly guiding us through the "heart." In Unification theology, God cannot rule by sheer law or power because love is voluntary, not forced. The Unification view explains that God as parent is centrally motivated by *shim-jung,* which might be translated from Korean as "deep heart." When we interpret this to mean "God is love," we Unificationists are not alone. There are some liberation theologians who see merit in calling God Father, if "Father" refers to love and mercy. For example, a Brazilian theologian has written: "Jesus incarnated the love and pardon of his Father, showing goodness and mercy to all; and he was particularly kind to those regarded as social or religious outcasts. This was not humanitarianism on Jesus' part. It was his way of making the Father's love concrete in his own life. If God himself is that way toward all, why shouldn't the Son of God act likewise?"[6]

In the above quotation, and many examples in Christian history, we find God, as love, showing mercy on sinful people. This has often been viewed as a type of love called *agape,*[7] or unconditional giving and forgiving love. *Agape* love is shown in the actions of Jesus Christ, especially his sacrifice for humanity on the cross. We find, then, that this concept of God as *agape* love has often become normative for Christian life.

However, this totally outgiving love generally means that the lover gives on his own initiation and his own terms. Without receiving input on how to love based on the receiver's perceived needs, this *agape* love can itself become paternalistic. Furthermore, there exists the problem of love for all people in general, and the depth of love that can be known in personal relationships. If each person is to strive for a model of *agape* love that contains a universal love for all human beings, with no relationships theoretically closer than any others, we encounter severe problems. Plato's *Republic* suggested that all children be held in common by the state and therefore be given the best instruction on becoming citizens. Aristotle criticized this view, arguing that the personal love children need could not be bureaucratically administered; it would become diluted. We have here what social scientists refer to as a "level of analysis" problem. Some Christians advocate a type of *agape* love that is blind to this problem. Although the motivation behind this type of love is noble, a love that is a general outpouring for all humanity is not sufficient in and of itself.

The belief in God as parent implies a different kind of love than that of a sacrificial, universal lover of the world. Unification theology views the love relationship between God and people as mutual, with both depending on love from each other for fulfillment of the heart or joy. A dynamic principle of giving and receiving is involved. Further, since all human life involves the principle of growth, in the earlier stages of one's life, one is more dependent on the parent than when one is developed. However, we cannot simply say that parents give and children receive. In Unification theology, we emphasize that both give and both receive or the relationship is only one way and, hence, not a relationship.

It follows, then, that God, if God is to have a relationship with humans, must be able to receive and feel joy as do God's children. Thus, a totally outgiving God, a God of sheer *agape,* is incomplete; a totally impassible God, beyond emotion, lacks a parental heart. The completion of the parent involves the completion of the children. Monastic life, so highly praised for its self-denial and sacrifice, is incomplete life. Families cannot be built on celibacy. Unification theology, which views relationships within the family as a basis for its ethics, cannot equate its *shim-jung* with Christian *agape.*

The Unification view sees God not only as a creator and a merciful redeemer, but as embodying all the qualities of ideal parents, masculine and feminine, including self-love and receiving love. To the extent that any developed nation could behave like God, in this view, toward the poorer nation, it would not act exploitatively in its own interest, but so as to nourish the development of the other. If a nation used the rhetoric of paternalism to provide a cover for exploitation, it would be evil. The critical issue is the nature of parenting, not the act itself.

But if God is ultimately the parent, then no nation can really occupy that position vis-à-vis other nations, except in some representative fashion. If God is parent, then nations are siblings. To delve into the economic implications of the doctrine that God is the parent of all human beings, we can turn to the question of the moral relationship between siblings.

God as Loving Parent Implies Nations Should Love Each Other

We can view the distinction between our relationship to our parent and that to our siblings as vertical and horizontal. The *Divine Principle,* the text of the Unification Church which interprets the Bible, places great emphasis on the fulfillment of both horizontal and vertical relationships.

In 1874, German theologian Albrecht Ritschl wrote a classic book titled *The Christian Doctrine of Justification and Reconciliation* in which he described the relationship between the Christian concept of justification and the ethics of the kingdom of God.[8] Ritschl, a father of modern liberal Christianity, is often remembered for his teaching Adolf von Harnack, a liberal theologian who advised Kaiser Wilhelm to go to war for the advancement of German civilization, the Christian concepts of "the Fatherhood of God, the Brotherhood of Man, and the Kingdom of God."[9] This is precisely the cliché against which feminist and liberation theologians react so vociferously. As a result, Ritschl's description of the relationship between faith and ethics is often overlooked.

Ritschl divided Christian teaching into two parts—dogmatics and ethics.[10] Dogmatics refers to presuppositions of divine operation, which leads to trust in God, and ethics refers to actions toward our neighbor. "Justification," which is a concept in the category of faith, is synonymous with the forgiveness of sins. To Ritschl this was the foundation stone of the Christian religion. However, he believed that the psychological side of religion, which deals with the subjective dimension of justification, is only part of religious life, a part in which all people initially stand equal before God. The dissimilarity and uniqueness of people existed, for him, under the scope of ethics.[11] He emphasized that faith or justification provides the basic attitude by which value judgments can be made by Christians. As such, religious ethics requires justification as a prerequisite to action.[12] The point is that, for Ritschl, ethics based on natural law theory or speculative philosophy or other forms of reasoned ethics are inadequate; one's attitude toward God, the object of faith, is of critical importance for human ethical relations.

Unification theology also divides human activity into this twofold scheme of vertical and horizontal religion. It does so with its teaching of the foundation of faith and the foundation of substance. The former compares to the traditional Christian doctrine of justification (faith) and the latter to sanctification (ethics). The vertical foundation of faith must be laid before horizontal ethical activity can have direct worth to God's kingdom on earth. The activity that we have as siblings therefore has ultimate worth insofar as it is grounded in the relationship with God, the parent of all.

Faith and national unity, in their perverse forms rooted in the quest for power for its own sake, were demanded by Adolf Hitler. Because of this and similar perversions, expressions of faith and unity are often looked upon with skepticism, if not abhorrence. Unification theology attempts to avoid coercive and exploitative perversions of faith by teaching that it must be seen as something given or extended by the faithful one, not something demanded by a person in a position of power. Similarly, unity should be seen as a bond of heart between people centered on God, and not some finite national or temporal objective. Anything short of this will result in either a tyranny by the person in power over the ruled, or a tyranny of a united group over other, less powerful, groups. The first case is an example of the false fatherhood against which the feminist and liberation theologians rebel; the second case, however, is the example of how a democracy, or a group in "solidarity" centered on a national goal, or an ideological goal such as a Marxist society, can be equally pernicious.

As perversion of parenthood does not eliminate the necessity of parenthood, the perversion of faith and unity do not mean the abandonment of their positive aspects. Unification theology requires, as did Ritschl, that world community centered on faith in God as our parent is required for the establishment of "the ideal world." In the language of the *Divine Principle,* the foundation of faith refers to the vertical and attitudinal aspect of the ideal world, and the foundation of substance refers to the horizontal unity among people and between people and the environment. To inherit God's blessings, people should (1) have the right attitude to receive God's blessings, and (2) be able to share God's blessings with one another. The attitude toward blessings, especially economic blessings, is one that is most immediate for our problem of the relationship between rich and poor nations. Indeed, in Unification theology, the attitude toward blessings given by God, our parent, lies at the center of the establishment of a world of harmony and peace; and thus, at the center of the relationship between rich and poor nations.

The Problem of a "Blessing"

A continual problem in human relationships is that which occurs when one person obtains something that another does not. This is the central problem in our discussion of the economic differential between rich and poor nations. The *Divine Principle* also sees this as a central problem in the relationship between siblings in the Bible. A blessing, if it is not received or used properly, will become a curse. For the person who obtains it becomes the target of the jealousy or vengeance of another. Cain killed Abel; and since the dawn of history thousands of lives have been lost because of resentment and jealousy. Certainly poor nations want to become rich; and rich nations want to retain their blessings. Attitudes of fear of loss and arrogance of power are dominant in rich nations. The seeds of resentment and jealousy are sown in the poor.

In the study of developing right relationships between sibling nations that are to share the blessings of God, the parent of all, the *Divine Principle* begins with the narrative of Cain and Abel, the first siblings in biblical history who confronted this problem. The *Divine Principle* then develops a Cain-and-Abel typology, which is used as a hermeneutical device in the study of human history. The approach can be compared to Hegel's tracing of the unfolding of the "Absolute Spirit" in history, or Marx's analysis of the stages of economic development. The *Divine Principle* traces the movement of history from the perspective it terms "God's Dispensation from the Standpoint of Restoration."[13] This concept involves the ability of human beings to receive and to share God's blessings.

Blessing, in whatever form, is something that is currently distributed unequally. The existence of this inequality breeds the attitudes that the *Divine Principle* describes as it interprets the biblical stories of Cain and Abel, and of Jacob and Esau. The relationship between Cain and Abel, rooted in attitudes of resentment and arrogance, represents failure; whereas the final reconciliation of Jacob and Esau, based on maturity, humility, and forgiveness, represents success. The story illustrates the transformation of "heart," or attitude, which was necessary for God-centered unity to be established between these two brothers so that both could prosper without quarrels over their father's inheritance making them enemies.

Understanding this dynamic between the biblical brothers can be applied to the relationship between rich and poor nations.

The Transformation from a "Fallen" to a "Restored" Attitude between Siblings

In Genesis 4, Abel sacrificed an offering that was acceptable to God, whereas Cain's offering was not accepted. Cain killed Abel because of jealousy, thus causing the first war in biblical history. This "war" was fought over the inheritance of God's blessing, but it showed little concern for God's parental point of view. The story tells us that attitudes with which brothers, or siblings, approach God's blessings have, since the beginning, been in drastic need of transformation. However, the Bible also teaches that this "fallen" nature can be overcome by humanity's return to God.

Abel, according to the *Divine Principle,* had de facto established a foundation of faith and was the channel through whom God could work to reach Cain. By faithfully sacrificing his offering, Abel had established a relationship of trust with God. The next step, therefore, was to establish the foundation of substance, the substantial reflection of his faith in God, which required ethical actions that would lead to the brothers' sharing of God's blessings.[14] The foundation of substance required that Cain and Abel unite in love and respect for each other. However, we read in the Bible that Cain was filled with resentment and jealousy and killed his brother Abel. Thus, the foundation of substance was not created in Adam's family. Cain, according to the *Divine Principle,* had repeated the fallen act of Lucifer by assuming a dominion over his brother that was not rightfully given to him by God; he attempted to gain a blessing by force rather than through love and respect.

The details of this ancient story are sketchy; we are not provided with an account of Abel's attitude toward Cain after his offering was accepted by God. However, we can speculate that Abel was at least partially at fault. It takes two people to make a relationship; both Cain and Abel had responsibilities based on their respective positions before God. Here, Abel had received a blessing from God. It was his providential duty to share this blessing with his brother Cain. However, we know that often when we receive a blessing of some kind or another we want to keep it for ourselves. If we take the attitude "No, it is mine, leave me alone!" or "What's wrong with you, how come you didn't get one!" then we will only aggravate the frustration of our Cain, who desperately wants the blessing himself. If we cannot properly share our blessings with our siblings, we fail as "true Abel" figures. A "fallen Cain" will have an attitude that will prompt him to attempt to seize a blessing by force if he cannot gain it with "Abel's" cooperation. Cain has a responsibility to seek a blessing as God would have him obtain it. If God's desire is for his human children to live harmoniously, then plunder by violence is condemned from God's point of view.

The *Divine Principle* teaches that there are Abel and Cain positions throughout the history of the "providence of restoration." In any relationship, one person stands in a position of having received a blessing from God, which the other has not received. The two, "Abel" and "Cain," have their respective responsibilities. According to the *Divine Principle,* only when a person with a restored Cain attitude unites with a person with a restored Abel attitude will the foundation of substance, which paves the way for the kingdom of God, be established.[15]

The *Divine Principle* traces the "foundation of faith" and the "foundation of substance" meticulously through the Bible. However, the paradigmatic story regarding the transformation of attitudes is found in the narrative of Jacob and Esau.

In Genesis 27, Jacob succeeded in receiving his father's blessing by tricking both his father and his brother Esau. Jacob caused a frustration for his brother Esau that recreated the tension over a blessing experienced by Cain and Abel two thousand biblical years earlier. Would this set of brothers succeed in creating a foundation of substance; or would they repeat the first murder? This question, according to the *Divine Principle,* is crucial in the unfolding of providential history.[16]

In this story, Esau became filled with anger against his brother Jacob just as Cain had responded toward Abel. We also find that Jacob, in Abel's position, had little compassion for his brother Esau. Thus, in the beginning of the story unity was impossible; Esau had adopted a "fallen Cain" attitude; Jacob had adopted a "fallen Abel" attitude. Jacob's blood would have been spilled on that day except for the providential intervention by the brothers' mother, Rebecca, who, on God's behalf as the parent had separated the two sons by sending Jacob to her brother in Haran. Thus, Jacob was not killed, but neither was he able to enjoy the blessing he had received from his father. Unity with Esau was the only way that that could be accomplished, or that God's desire for the siblings to share God's blessings could be established.

Reading further in the story, we find that Jacob himself was deceived several times as he worked for his uncle Laban, who sought to exploit him. However, Jacob did not respond with a fallen Cain attitude, welling up with anger or resentment, or seeking to kill his uncle. He patiently served and creatively worked to gain his freedom at the cost of twenty-one years of sacrifice and patience.[17] Eventually he prevailed and was blessed by Laban with many possessions; and, at the Ford of Jabbok, he was blessed by God and given the name Israel, which means "victorious one."

Through his experience in Haran, it is likely that Jacob came to understand how his brother Esau had felt when he had been tricked. Jacob approached his brother with a new attitude by offering his possessions, and ultimately himself, to his brother. This condition of love moved Esau's heart so that he put down his weapons and embraced his brother Jacob. This was the union God had been waiting for since the dawn of history. The hearts of Jacob and Esau had been reoriented; Esau and Jacob were able to love each in the context of stewardship over the blessings they had received. On this foundation, and with this transformed attitude, Israel was prepared to receive God's blessings on the national level. The passage that reflects the transformed attitudes follows:

> And Jacob lifted up his eyes and looked, and behold, Esau was coming, and four hundred men with him. . . .He himself went on before [his party], bowing to the ground seven times, until he came near his brother. But Esau ran to meet him, and embraced him, and fell on his neck and kissed him. . . .Esau said, "What do you mean by all this company which I met?" Jacob answered, "To find favor in the sight of my lord." But Esau said, "I have enough my brother; keep what you have for yourself." Jacob said, "No, I pray you, if I have found favor in your sight, then accept my present from my hand; for truly to see your face is like seeing the face of God, with such favor you have received me.[18]

Sibling Relations Among the Nations

Today, when we look at the emotional strife and the rhetoric between rich and poor nations, we see some of the same attitudes that are discussed in the biblical stories. The fallen attitudes between siblings are not treated by political scientists or economists from the religious viewpoint of redemption, or transformation, described above. It is my contention that, until the religious implication of the concept of the siblinghood of nations with God as parent is addressed, the internal problem of the relationship between rich and poor nations cannot be remedied.

In April 1980, Reverend Moon, the founder of the Unification Church, spoke about unity between the rich and the poor of the world. Here is an excerpt from his talk that reflects the application of the transformed attitude in sharing God's blessings in the current world situation:

> With the 1980's we move to the national level dispensation. People need to acquire a cosmopolitan world ideology. Neither communism nor democracy have manifested this cosmopolitanism. Democracy is failing America and communism has exposed its lack of respect for human life. In the communist world people are eliminated for the sake of ideology. Democracy is fittest for high class people and has failed to embrace the lower classes. . . .Communism sympathizes with the lower classes and their struggles but makes enemies with the upper classes, cutting them off completely. From God's point of view, there is a better possibility in working through democracy; because the democratic world makes information available, while the communist world makes clandestine decisions. God favors the way of openness.
>
> A new thought must absorb and digest these two ideologies. In this new approach, the upper class should come down and be a servant of the lower class. . . .Christianity itself has become weak and often sympathizes with the communist view. Thus, when they come down to the oppressed, they join "the other side" and cut themselves off from the channels by which they could lift the people up. . . .
>
> God's way is always unity. God's thought can embrace both the upper and lower classes and elevate the entire society to a higher standard of living. . . .The Unification Church declares no enemy; it embraces everyone and saves everyone. The means it uses is love; God's love. . . .
>
> The tradition of the Unification Church must first be established. When the foundation is laid, a blessing can be given out. First, we need an economic foundation and a strong educational system that can overcome evil ideologies. Then we can embrace the world, listening to the lower class as well as the upper.[19]

Nations exist in the same world created by God. From this viewpoint, political attitudes of nations should be consistent with the ideal of the kingdom of God in which people live as brothers and sisters. National decisions and policies greatly affect the fate of God's children and the blessings God has given. Nations are not sovereign from a global perspective, but as actors they have a responsibility to assist the inheritance of God's blessings by all people.

If we review the stories of Cain and Abel and Jacob and Esau, we find that "inheritance" or "stewardship" of blessings requires an attitude of trust and care. It involves the attitude of children who are to take care of, and make flourish, the world their parent bestowed on them. As such, qualities of character and abilities are required in order to receive a blessing. It is important to note that a simplistic view that would equally divide the material resources of the world, counting each person as one, regardless of attitude or ability, is opposed by this Unification concept of blessing. Therefore, some of the ideals of equality current in both democratic and communist societies are not sustained by the Unification position. Unification sees all God's children as equally dear and precious, but it does not necessarily see that each person, by virtue of becoming eighteen or twenty-one years of age, is equally qualified to inherit God's blessings. There is an "elitism of stewardship" implied in the concept that the person closest to God's heart is in the position to channel God's blessings to other siblings.

Although there are strong, often violently revolutionary, tendencies to establish "democratic" societies in which all people have an equal share of power and wealth, this ideal of equality seldom adequately considers the responsibilities of stewardship from God's point of view. When violence, based on resentment or jealousy, is fomented by political movements, they must be classified by Unification theology as a fallen Cain type.

At this point it is important to transcend the suspicion that Unification theology is building a case to support the conservative military regimes of the Third World by saying that revolutionary violence represents fallen Cain behavior and should be suppressed. Leaders and rulers of the upper classes, or democratic economies that stand in a position to control wealth, are as susceptible to fallen nature as the poor. A democratic structure in itself will not cure fallen nature. In the United States, each person of voting age counts as one equal share of voting power. However, what was the requirement of stewardship, what was the test of leadership, character, ability, to become a voter? Simply that he or she physically reached the age of eighteen or twenty-one. The historical track record is clear: as individuals United States citizens do not like to oppress people, as naive voters they listen to promises by political candidates who can only fulfill their promise of riches at home by exploiting someone abroad. Thus, people of the United States stand in a contradiction; they like to view themselves as good Christians in their personal lives, but as a structural collective they perpetrate injustice beyond their borders. The ideals of the democratic movement that sought to balance and correct power in the United States by division of power was valuable in that it sought to give value to each person as a child of God; it was limited in that it did not produce qualified stewards of God's world—it has often produced naive voters. These naive voters, people who have inherited blessings, who have riches or power at their control and improperly use them, must be considered fallen Abel types by Unification theology as we have construed it.

In this fallen world, the world separated from God, we find that the left-wing revolutionaries, who fight to gain "blessings," represent a fallen Cain attitude, and the right-wing conservatives, who desire to hold onto their "blessings," generally represent a fallen Abel attitude. According to Unification theology, neither of these attitudes represents God's parental point of view. These attitudes must be transformed, as was the case with Jacob and Esau.

On the national level, the restoration of "heart," which Jacob and Esau experienced, is translated into national goals, structure, and policy. It is not enough to have kind-hearted people; national structure perpetuates its own goals. In the United States, without voter responsibility there will continue to be irresponsible national policies arrived at through "politicization" rather than sound political thought. It is likely that the people of the United States will have to go through their own Haran, if they have not learned the traditional lessons of overcoming fallen sibling attitudes. We could say that Americans are often naive in a way similar to Abel and Jacob.

Rich and poor nations are siblings; one has been in control of material blessings, the other has not. The control of riches in itself does not imply that God has blessed the nation (contrary to some Calvinist theology). Both types of nations have their respective responsibilities. Rich nations and poor nations alike are required to cultivate the attitudes and skills necessary to attain God's blessings on the inheritance he has given the world.

Rich nations may have to experience their "Haran" before they can empathize with the plight of the poor and create an attitude of concern that the poor can accept. Poor nations are required to suppress their resentment or jealousy as they seek nonthreatening ways of acquiring economic blessings. They must still be able to see the people of rich nations as their siblings, even though the rich have often manipulated them. Although the context may differ, the principle of unity of heart among siblings remains firm. Particular strategies or programs of cooperation, though essential, are less important than fundamental attitudes as brothers and sisters toward the blessings of God, our parent.

NOTES

1. Mary Daly, *Beyond God the Father: Toward a Philosophy of Women's Liberation* (Boston: Beacon Press, 1973).
2. Joseph Comblin, "What Sort of Service Might Theology Render?," *Frontiers of Theology in Latin America,* ed. Rosino Gibellini (New York: Orbis Books, 1979), 70–71.
3. Edward Shils, *Tradition* (Chicago: University of Chicago Press, 1981), 6–8, 33.
4. *Divine Principle,* p. 488; "The Jesus-type person on the Satanic side [in the Second World War] was Hitler."
5. Ibid., 22–39.
6. Leonardo Boff, "Christ's Liberation via Oppression," *Frontiers of Theology in Latin America,* 122.
7. Anders Nygren has given the most detailed exposition of *agape* in Christian history in his *Agape and Eros,* trans. Philip S. Watson (London: S.P.C.K., 1953).
8. Albrecht Ritschl, *The Christian Doctrine of Justification and Reconciliation* (Edinburgh: T.&T. Clark, 1902).
9. See Adolf von Harnack, *What Is Christianity?,* trans. T. B. Saunders (Gloucester, MA: Peter Smith Pub., 1978).
10. Ritschl, *The Christian Doctrine,* 14, 333.
11. Ibid., 198.
12. Ibid., 203–6.
13. *Outline of the Principle, Level 4,* 101–4.
14. Ibid., 120–21.
15. "Though Cain and Abel stood on the sides of good and evil respectively, their positions are relative. Actually, both had Original Sin and Fallen Nature as well as Original Nature." Ibid., 118n.
16. Ibid., 135–37.
17. In Unification theology this sacrifice is called "indemnity," a less than co-

herent concept concerned that suffering done is not abstract but for "God's purpose." *Divine Principle,* pp. 222–27. See also, *Restoring the Kingdom,* ed. Deane William Ferm (New York: Paragon House, 1984).

18. Genesis 33:1–11.
19. Notes from an unpublished speech given by Reverend Moon to a gathering in his home, April 27, 1980.

Part Three

GOD OF THE POOR AND OPPRESSED

9

God of the Rich, God of the Poor

RITA H. MATARAGNON

Is the God of the rich the same God as the God of the poor? Do the rich and the poor see the same images and qualities of God? Do they worship God and express their religiosity in the same way? Do they perceive their lives to be controlled to the same extent by God?

Far from being obvious, the relationship between religion and social class has often been controversial and equivocal. Earlier ideas about religion leaned toward an independence between religion and social class.[1] Theologically, God was portrayed as a transcendent being "out there" to be sought, rather than a presence or a meaning to be experienced in social reality. Sociologically, religion was seen as serving a solidarity function through its creation and protection of a common set of values. As Emile Durkheim defined it, religion is "a unified system of beliefs and practices related to sacred things, that is to say, things set apart and forbidden—beliefs and practices which unite into one single moral community called a church, all those who adhere to them. Collective worship binds men with a force above and beyond them; it is this moral force that regulates social relationships and curbs deviance."[2]

If one religion could unite, then different religions or even different interpretations of one religion could divide. Thus, religious wars and schisms result. Different religions also make different pronouncements about suffering, well-being, merit, and the importance or unimportance of this world vis-à-vis the next. Such pronouncements invariably have important consequences on how the adherents of a particular religion view and tolerate class differences. On the other hand, it is also recognized that wealth and status can influence the acceptance of religious beliefs and practices. As in the case of the rich young man who sought Jesus, it was said that he went away sorrowful when asked to sell all he had for the poor, for he had great possessions.[3]

In this century, interest in the relationship between religion and social class has been spurred by macrocomparisons of the worldly success enjoyed by groups professing different religions. Max Weber, in relating religious beliefs and practices (economic ethics), presented evidence for a functional relationship between Calvinist Protestantism and a speedy advance of some countries toward capitalism in the sixteenth and seventeenth centuries (e.g., the Huguenots of the Netherlands, the Puritans of New England, and parts of Germany).[4] Calvinists ascribe a positive ethical and religious value to work (the Protestant work ethic); since work is seen as an instrument to glorify God, wealth that results from work is taken as God's blessing.[5]

Later critics, notably K. Samuelsson, have cast doubt on Weber's correlation between Calvinism and capitalism by pointing to other reasons for the speedy capitalist development in the countries cited.[6] Samuelsson also pointed to cases where Calvinism took hold but was not coupled with speedy capitalist development (e.g., Scotland and Hungary) and to cases where capitalism did develop but was not associated with Calvinist beliefs (e.g., England and Sweden).

Studies on the role of religion in social mobility within a complex society such as the United States have also met with similar problems. The fact that different religious groups are often also racially and culturally different naturally precludes a clear relationship and points to the need for microcomparisons among social classes found within a single (preferably small and homogenous) society bound by a common religion.

The position that religion is related to social class *within* a class society has not lacked intuitive or theoretical appeal. Marx and Engels considered religion to be an opiate and a fantasy escape from suffering for the masses.[7] In this way, religion was believed to serve the interest of the bourgeoisie in fostering complacency and preventing class antagonism.

Quite apart from any Machiavellian intention to manipulate, religion is seen to vary across social classes simply because different class groups have different inherent needs. Weber has theorized extensively on the religion of the privileged and the nonprivileged classes within a society. Regardless of the content of the religion, the need of the poor is for salvation and release from suffering, whereas the need of the rich is for legitimation (merit) of privilege and psychological assurance of worth.[8]

Not only needs, but also interests, expectations, customs, thought categories, forms of expression, and behavior make up the experience of social reality. "Hence the variation, from one social class to another, of the religious undertakings that are possible or impossible, undesirable even though possible, tolerable but up to a point (a different point in each class), acceptable but just barely, important, basic or urgent."[9]

According to Susan Budd, "that religious beliefs and practices systematically vary by social class is indisputable."[10] Even among Catholic congregations working in a fixed tradition there may be observed variations in mood, decorations, and the way in which priest and congregation are related in worship. There is a difference, too, in the type of religious activity practiced. In both Britain and the United States, higher rates of *private* religious practice—private prayer and Bible reading—are reported by the poor, and higher rates of *public* worship by the upper middle class. In doctrine, the lower class is more fundamentalist, lays greater emphasis on a literal Bible, sin, and afterlife, and is more devout and knowledgeable about the Bible than the middle class. For the upper middle class, religion is more of an ethical matter, and the right to self-determination of religious beliefs is therefore emphasized. In the United States, the denominations of the upper middle class have a liberal theology with stress on individual ethical conduct; the denominations of the poor are predominantly theologically conservative.[11]

The orthodox and conservative posture of the poor is said to be related to Marx and Engel's theory about alienation and religion. "Religious belief, the acceptance of particular dogmas and particular codes of behavior as absolutely and ultimately true, is more typical of the exploited class rather than of their oppressors; their lack of property, and therefore of command over the circumstances of their lives, is reflected in their religious submissiveness."[12]

The differences observed have been those of the First World, during the last few decades. Today, many changes are taking place in religion, especially in the Third World. As Ugalde puts it,

> The Left has long since issued its condemnation of religion. The Right, by contrast, has spent the last decade revising some of its traditional certitudes. There used to be a kind of agreement on both sides that religion is the solid stanchion of the established order, good for nothing but the ideology of the dominating class. But today, in Latin America, this class is itself beginning to denounce the church as "subversive and revolutionary."[13]

In the Philippines, particularly in Metro Manila, various developments in recent years have left their imprint on elements of the local Catholic church, possibly disproportionately across the different social classes. These developments include the shift to less ritualized forms of worship, the encouragement of private religious practices such as Bible reading and private prayer, the new tolerance for and understanding of folk religion, the emergence of liberation theology, and the recent charismatic movement. How, then, do the different social classes now view God and religion?

Although many statements about class differences in religious beliefs and practices have been based on sporadic and anecdotal observations and experiences, and occasionally on church reports, this exploratory study attempts a systematic investigation of class differences on various important aspects of religion: images and perceived qualities of God; dimensions of religiosity including religious beliefs, closeness to God, religious practices, knowledge of religious doctrine, consequence of religion on behavior; and locus of control (God versus self). The study is deliberately confined to a small geographic area in which reside members of different social classes, but which is otherwise homogenous in most other respects, including church influence and accessibility. Rather than test hypotheses, the study aims to investigate whether de facto class differences exist in the religious beliefs and practices explored. The results of this study, aside from showing yet another aspect of class differences, are expected to have serious implications for those involved in religious work.

Method, Site, and Sample

Katipunan was chosen as a small urban area in which residents of different social classes live. Although there are cases in which a plush residence lies side by side with a group of makeshift shanties, generally the whole Katipunan area consists of varied and disparate communities whose social class could be easily identified. The three types of residential communities represented in the study are the following: privately developed, plush, and exclusive residential subdivisions such as La Vista, Blue Ridge, White Plains, Loyola Heights, and Xavierville for the upper middle class; middle-class areas such as Project 4, Balara, Aurora Boulevard, and Katipunan Road (the first two are government housing projects); and large squatter areas such as Barrio Escopa, Pansol, and Marytown for the lower class. Although some communities have small chapels within them, all of the communities are covered by two major parishes, St. Joseph's and Santa Maria della Strada's.

The sampling frame of this study consisted of all Catholic Filipinos residing in Katipunan. Stratified random sampling was used to ensure that the various subcommunities within each class were represented. Inasmuch as educational achievement was expected to be correlated with economic status, it was next to impossible to separate the two variables. However, since it was also expected that any variance in education would most likely be found within the middle class, the middle class was divided into those with college education (Class B) and those without college education (Class C). In this way, if Class C behaved more like Class B, economic status could be judged the more influential variable, but if Class C behaved more like the lower class (Class D), then education would be considered more influential.

A total of 194 respondents aged thirty to forty-five were interviewed for this study. The breakdown in terms of social class and sex follows:

Class	Description	Number of Males	Number of Females	Total Number
A	Upper-middle class	25	26	51
B	Middle class with college education	23	25	48
C	Middle class without college education	24	22	46
D	Lower class	20	29	49
				194

Research Instrument

Through research of related literature and preliminary unstructured interviews with Catholics, a questionnaire to answer the research problem was prepared originally in English and later translated to Filipino. A few items were adapted from existing questionnaires on religiosity and many others were original.[14] A theology professor was consulted for the sections on creed and knowledge of doctrine.

The final questionnaire consisted of the following parts:

Images and Qualities of God

1. Free Association (1 item)
   Description: the question asked, "When you think of God, what characteristic of God comes first to your mind? God is———."
2. Choice of Two Most Important Attributes of God (1 item)
   Description: a list of eighteen commonly cited attributes (adjectives) of God were presented from which the respondent had to choose two adjectives he or she considered most important in describing God. Examples: powerful, merciful, holy, loving, protective, strong, just, etc.
3. Drawing or Representation of God (1 item)
   Description: the question asked, "If you were asked to draw a picture of God, or a picture to represent God, what would you draw?" It was emphasized that artistic ability was not important; in fact, both pictures and verbal descriptions were permitted.

Dimensions of Religiosity

1. Creed or Beliefs (12 items)
   Description: items expressed religious beliefs (some orthodox, some not) and were followed by five-point scales ranging from "strongly disagree" to "strongly agree." Themes included eternal life, divinity of Christ, Scripture as God's Word, man's accountability to God, man's need for God, salvation, miracles, Immaculate Conception, repentance, etc. Examples: (a) I believe Jesus Christ was an exceptionally good man, but not God. (b) I believe that Virgin Mary was conceived without sin.
2. Closeness to God (12 items)
   Description: items described different kinds of personal religious experience that indicated either closeness to God (positive religious experience) or distance from God (negative religious experience). Themes included personal prayer, trust in God, security against death, religion giving purpose to life, etc. Items were followed by five-point scales ranging from "strongly disagree" to "strongly agree." Examples: (a) Whenever I have problems, I turn to God for help. (b) I find God too abstract and distant to affect my life directly.
3. Regular Religious Practices (18 items)
   Description: this section presented a list of rituals and activities

that Catholics could perform at any time of the year. Each activity was followed with eight variations of frequency, ranging from "never" to "daily." Examples: (a) Pray the rosary. (b) Give to the collection. (c) Join a charismatic meeting. (Note: private personal prayer was not classified in this section on rituals since it was dealt with in the section on closeness to God.)

4. Seasonal Religious Practices (18 items)
   Description: these were rituals and activities that Catholics could perform once a year, for a special season. Most of them had to do with the Lenten Season. Each activity was followed with eight variations of frequency ranging from "never" to "daily." Examples: (a) Read the *Pasyon.* (b) Receive ashes on Ash Wednesday. (c) Attend the *Misa de Gallo* (Advent Mass).
5. Practices that Make One Feel Closest to God (1 item)
   Description: respondent was asked to choose from the eighteen regular and eighteen seasonal practices which five activities he or she could rank as making him or her feel closest to God.
6. Knowledge of Religion (10 items)
   Description: multiple-choice items concerning Catholic doctrine were used. Themes included definition of salvation, Immaculate Conception, Advent, etc.; recognition of four gospels, sacraments of initiation, etc. Examples: Immaculate Conception means (a) Mary conceived Jesus Christ without sin. (b) Mary conceived Jesus Christ while remaining a virgin. (c) Mary was born without sin. (d) Mary was conceived without sin.
7. Consequence on Behavior (8 items)
   Description: items were statements expressing the "rightness" or "wrongness" of certain actions. Each one is followed by a five-point scale ranging from "strongly disagree" to "strongly agree." Examples: (a) If a neighbor meets with an emergency and asks for help, it is your Christian duty to do so even if you have to sacrifice your savings. (b) It is all right for a Catholic young man and a Catholic young woman in love to have premarital sex.

Locus of Control/Responsibility (10 items)

1. *Description:* each item consisted of one pair of statements, one of which attributed locus of control to God, the other to self. Respondent had to choose from each pair of statements which one he or she agreed with *more.* Examples: (a) In the long run

God makes sure the bad things that happen to us are balanced by the good ones. (b) Most misfortunes are the result of lack of ability, ignorance, laziness, or all three.

Procedure

Respondents, all residents of Katipunan, were contacted at home and asked if they could be interviewed about their views and opinions on religion and on God. The interview was presented as part of a research project surveying people's attitudes on God and religion. Confidentiality and anonymity were assured. The respondent's name was not asked; however, his or her religion, age, and educational background were. The language facility and preference of the respondent was considered, and so English was used for Classes A and B, Filipino for Classes C and D. Interviewers refrained from identifying their own religious affiliation and activities to prevent any untoward influence on the respondent. The whole interview typically took about forty-five minutes. Although respondents who insisted on self-administering their own questionnaire were permitted to do so, the interviewing format was basically preserved with the interviewer's close supervision, instructions, occasional probing, and check for completion of responses after each section of the questionnaire.

Results

Two images of God emerged most strongly: the benevolent God (loving, kind, merciful, etc.) and the powerful God (strong, majestic, powerful, etc.). Class A respondents distinctly saw God as more benevolent than any other group. Most dimensions of religiosity were also directly correlated with social status. People with higher social status were more religious on these dimensions: creed, closeness to God, seasonal rituals, and knowledge of doctrine. Finally, the different social classes were not significantly different in terms of their locus-of-control orientation, although significant differences were obtained for some specific items.

Images of God

Free Association. Although there were various idiosyncratic answers, the majority of answers could be categorized into two clusters of qualities about God. One cluster could be identified as the benevolent God (generous, kind, good, loving, merciful, understanding, forgiving, etc.). Another cluster could be identified as the powerful God (great, supreme, almighty, above all, etc.). For this free-association section, the majority of the spontaneous answers, especially for Class A, fell into the category of the benevolent God (102 responses), whereas the other qualities of God took a back seat (58 responses for "powerful" category, less than 10 responses for all other categories such as "life," "everlasting," "holy," "wise," "father/creator," and "peace/security/light." It is interesting to note that more of the "security" answers came from Class D). A chi-square analysis, which took into account only the two biggest categories (powerful versus benevolent), showed a marginally significant association between social class and category of association. This was mainly due to the fact that more than three times as many Class A respondents gave a benevolent association rather than a powerful one. Classes B, C, and D were not very different from one another.

Choice of Important Attributes. On this item, the positive relationship between social class and perception of God as benevolent showed up much more clearly. A highly significant X^2 value ($X^2 = 12.78$, p less than .01) was obtained. The four social classes were neatly arranged in terms of their benevolent versus powerful choices. For Class A, more than twice as many respondents chose "benevolent" adjectives rather than "powerful" ones; for Class B, the split was about equal; for Class C, slightly more chose the "powerful" adjectives; and for Class D, significantly more chose "powerful" adjectives over "benevolent" ones.

Drawings/Representations of God. The most common of the drawings depicted conventional religious symbols such as a cross, a heart, the Sacred Heart, a chalice and host, and the ci-ro symbol. Among these, the cross was most commonly depicted. Class D had the highest percentage of respondents (28.5 percent) who used a cross to represent God; it was also the only group who drew pictures of the Sacred Heart (12 percent). The next two most common representations were persons and nature scenes. Persons were commonly depicted as happy (smiling), loving (set in a heart or with heart aflame), giving or forgiving (arms outstretched), and generally with kind and gentle expressions. These were also the most common expressions for the less than 10 percent who attempted to draw God (nonpersons with angels nearby, bearded figures on thrones) or Jesus (as historically portrayed). An interesting observation is that for drawings either of persons or of God/Jesus, Class C and Class D had more themes of sorrow, suffering, and pain. These are expressed with arrows shot at a heart, a crown of thorns, a man nailed to a cross, a bleeding heart, etc. Nature scenes (e.g., sun, moon, stars, trees, mountains) were most popular with Class B (20.8 percent), followed by Class C (10.8 percent). Only 2 percent from Classes A, B, and C tried to represent the just God (e.g., a scale, hammer used by judge).

Creed or Belief. The most strongly held belief was the belief that "God can perform miracles if he wants to" (x=4.60 on a five-point scale), followed by the belief that God is a heavenly father who created man and to whom man is accountable. The negatively phrased items, although reversed in scoring, generally received lower ratings, suggesting the presence of an acquiescence response set, which was, however, not specific to any one group. The lowest-scoring item was belief concerning God's action in human history.

A significant difference was obtained only between Class A and Class C for the creed. On specific items, the lower classes (C and D) showed more doubt about the divinity of Christ (item 2) and about personal accountability to God as creator and heavenly father (item 4). Class A differed significantly from Class C and Class D on the matter of Christ's divinity. Class A also differed significantly from Class D on the revelation of God's Word through the Scriptures (item 3), whereas Class A and Class B differed significantly from Class C on personal accountability and on nature as God (item 10). In all differences, it was the higher social class that showed more agreement with the orthodox Catholic belief. Males and females showed no differences in religious beliefs except on one item: females believed more strongly in eternal life.

Closeness to God. Among various statements indicating closeness to God, respondents were most inclined to agree that they turn to God for help whenever they have problems (x=4.38). Many respondents also consider private prayer an important and satisfying aspect of their religious experience (x=4.35).

Class differences in closeness to God are very impressive. Statistically, this dimension of religiosity yielded the highest degree of class differences (F=4.71, p=.004). On the whole, Class A felt significantly "closer to God" than both Class C and Class D. Significant differences were obtained for seven of the twelve items. Class A was significantly different from Class D on the matter of religion in offering a sense of security in the face of death decreased steadily as one went down the social ladder. Class D respondents found God more abstract than all other groups, especially Class A respondents. Perhaps the most pathetic difference for Class D was reflected in their agreement with the item "When I pray, I feel as if my prayers do not reach God." On this item Class D differed significantly from all other groups! Class C and to some extent Class D were most inclined to agree with the statement that "Religion is good for some people, but personally it does not mean much to me." Belief in the sufficiency of one's own morality and conscience as guide (no need for regular prayer and Bible reading) increased as social status decreased. Trust in God despite temporary problems was surprisingly less for the middle classes, especially B, than for Class A and Class D.

Males and females were found to be significantly different in their overall closeness to God. Females also rated significantly higher on these particular items:

"Whenever I have problems, I turn to God for help."

"During the happiest moments in my life, I feel the presence of God."

"Private prayer is an important and satisfying aspect of my religious experience."

"I feel that I can trust God in the long run even if he gives me temporary problems."

"Most of the time I feel quite close to God."

Religious Practices. Although there were no significant class differences in overall scores of regular religious activities (all eighteen practices taken together), there were significant class differences on some specific practices:

read the Bible	A > D[15]
pray for sick and dead	A > BDC, B > DC
go to mass	AB > CD
take communion	A > BCD
visit the sick	BCD > A
give to collection	ABC > D
fast, abstain for religious reason	AB > C

Among all regular religious practices, the conventional Sunday-related public worship activities seem to be most frequent: mass, followed by communion, then by giving to the collection. Praying for the sick and the dead comes next, followed by a far fifth for Bible reading. No overall sex differences were obtained, but females were significantly more frequent in their Bible reading, praying for the sick/dead, praying the rosary, taking communion, making novenas, and offering flowers.

For seasonal (yearly) activities, higher frequency was correlated with higher social status. The activities on which the different social classes differed were the following:

read the Bible during Holy Week	ABC > D
read the Pasyon	D > CBA
do the Stations of the Cross	ABC > D
fast/abstain on Ash Wednesday	AB > CD
go for confession during Holy Week	A > CD
have communion on Easter Sunday	A > CD
make sacrifices or *penitencia* (aside from fasting)	A > CD
receive ash on Ash Wednesday	A > CD, B > D
wear scapular medal	A > B, A > D
wear black/purple clothes during Lent	D > BA, C > A
do visita iglesia	A > CD, B > D
attend Misa de Gallo (Advent Mass)	A > D
participate in block rosary	BC > AD

Among all the seasonal religious practices, having communion on Easter Sunday rated the highest frequency, followed by receiving ash on Ash Wednesday, then by fasting and abstaining on Good Friday. Other high-frequency activities were reading the Bible, going for confession, and doing stations of the cross during Holy Week.

Activities Fostering Closeness to God. Despite the proliferation of religious practices in the Philippines, it appears that nothing can take the place of mass. Attending mass ranked highest as the activity that brought one closer to God for all groups except Class A, which ranked it second to communion (still in the context of mass). Taking communion, reading the Bible, and praying the rosary were the next most effective practices that made respondents feel close to God. For these basic activities there were no apparent class differences in their overall basic effectiveness. However, for the fifth rank some class differences showed up. Going to confession was a frequent choice of Classes A and B, and so was doing the stations of the cross for Class A. On the other hand, making novenas made it to the top five for Class D.

Knowledge of Religion

The relationship between knowledge of religion and social status was practically linear (A greater than B greater than C greater than D). Religiosity as shown in knowledge about one's own religion is obviously a pure function of general education, as far as Filipinos are concerned. Both Class A and Class B differed significantly from Class D. Males and females did not differ significantly on knowledge of religion.

Among the items in the multiple-choice knowledge test, the one with the most correct answers (75.8 percent) was the item about Jesus Christ being true God and true man. This was followed by a far second for the mystery of the Trinity (63.4 percent), the four gospels (62.7 percent), and the meaning of Advent. On the other hand, fewest correct answers were obtained for the item on Immaculate Conception (27.3 percent) and for the mystery of the church (32.5 percent).

Consequence in Behavior. Adherence to the moral teachings of the church was neither affected by class per se nor by sex per se. However, a significant interaction effect between social class and sex was obtained. For Class A, female respondents were stricter in their adherence to moral teachings of the church, whereas in Class D, it was the male respondents who showed higher scores than the females! Class B and Class C had nearly equal scores for males and females, with some slight tendency for females in Class B to be higher and males in Class C to be higher. All in all, Class A females had the highest scores and Class D females had the lowest scores. Among the females, the ranked order would be A, B, C, D; but among the males, the ranked order would be D, C, A, B.

	Female	Male
A	30.54	28.52
B	29.88	28.39
C	29.32	29.38
D	26.78	30.04

For specific items two were found to be significantly affected by social class. One was, "Although I believe in religion, I refuse to let religious considerations influence my everyday life." Class D was most likely to agree with this item, indicating a lack of religious influence on behavior. Class A, scoring highest, differed significantly from Class C and Class D; even Class B differed significantly from Class D.

A second item affected by social class was the stand on family planning. The item read, "A couple have had four and would like to limit their family. Since the couple prefer a most effective method, it is justified for the woman to take the pill."[16] Here again, Class D was least inclined to adhere to church teaching. Thus, a significant difference was obtained between Class D and Classes A and B.

Maximum agreement (x=4.14) was registered for the item on obedience to God's moral laws: "True love of God is shown in obedience to his moral laws." Apart from this, the two highest scores were associated with moral judgments that had to do with interpersonal relationships—helping a neighbor in need and forgiving those who wrong us.

Locus of Control

Contrary to expectation, locus-of-control scores did not differ significantly according to social class. Surprisingly, though, clear patterns of differences were found for eight of the ten items (five highly significant and three marginally significant). An examination of these specific items explains why an overall difference could not possibly be found. Different items took different *directions* of differences, suggesting the multidimensionality of the locus-of-control construct.

On three items, higher control was positively associated with higher social status. No exceptions were found for these three items for which the scores ranked neatly from A (highest) to D (lowest). The higher the social class, the more likely the respondent was to agree with the following statements:

"What happens to me is my own doing."[17]

"Becoming a success is really a matter of hard work."

"When I make plans, I am almost certain that I can make them work."

An examination of the three items suggests an assertion of confidence about one's lot, success, and plans carrying out.

On two items, higher control was inversely associated with social class, i.e., the lower social class had higher scores. Class D was most inclined to agree with the following two items:

> "Most misfortunes are the result of inability, ignorance, laziness, or all three."

> "I pray that God will give me strength to accomplish more for his glory."

The above two items seem to have little in common except an acknowledgement of failure and an attempt to do more.

On three items, the two middle classes showed a distinct difference from the two extreme classes (BC versus AD). For the following two items, both Classes B and C, especially B, scored higher than Classes A and D (B and C greater than A and D):

> "A person can have a happy life if he or she works for it."

> "I have found that God helps those who help themselves."

These two items express a simple belief in self-help and happiness, but without the same confidence of Class A.

Finally, for the item on political involvement, Classes B and C differed from Classes A and D in their pessimism about control over social change (B and C less than A and D):

> "By taking active part in political and social affairs, people can indirectly affect public events."

Males and females did not show any difference on any of the locus of control items.

Summary of Results

1. The higher the social class, the more respondents saw God as benevolent.
2. The lower the social class, the more respondents saw God as powerful.
3. The higher the social class, the more respondents expressed belief in the official Catholic creed.
4. The higher the social class, the more respondents (especially women) expressed a feeling of closeness to God.
5. Although there was no significant difference in overall frequency of all religious activities, the most conventional church

activities (e.g., mass, communion, and giving to collection) enjoyed more frequent practice as social status increased.

6. The higher the social class, the more respondents (especially women) observed seasonal religious activities.
7. The higher the social class, the more knowledge respondents had about their religion.
8. No general class of sex differences were found for adherence to moral teachings. However, for the upper middle class, females show more adherence to moral teachings than males, whereas for the lower class, females show less adherence than males.
9. Females were significantly more religious than males on certain dimensions of religiosity: closeness to God and frequency of seasonal religious practices.
10. There was no significant difference in overall locus-of-control scores. However, significant differences in perceived control were obtained for many specific items, except that the direction of difference was not uniform, suggesting a multidimensional variable.

Discussion

The God of the rich is perceived to be more benevolent (kind, loving, caring, forgiving, etc.) than the God of the poor. Belief in him and in his divine revelation is stronger, emotional ties to him are closer, more religious practices are carried out for him, and more knowledge about him and his inspired doctrine is transmitted.

On the other hand, the God of the poor is perceived to be more powerful (strong, majestic, above all, etc.) than the God of the rich. This attribute may explain his distance, since the poor express less proximity to God. Being distant, it is no wonder that the God of the poor is somewhat hard of hearing. The poor are most likely to believe that their prayers do not reach God. However, for the minority, who might identify more closely with God, they see him as a suffering God or Christ (bleeding heart, arrow through heart, crucifix). This preference for the image of the suffering Christ is consistent with the poor's devotion to the *Pasyon*. Reynaldo Ileto even credited the *Pasyon* with providing the inspiration for the Philippine revolution, since the suffering Christ was courageous and able to overcome suffering, emerging victorious over his enemies.[18]

The God of the poor seems to inspire a less orthodox and compelling system of beliefs and doctrine; there is more of a tendency to put him aside or on a pedestal rather than to let him influence everyday life. Personal morality and conscience are perceived to be adequate substitutes for regular prayer and Bible reading. Practical concern and empathy, rather than official church teaching, guide the judgment of the poor about family planning. Perhaps because he is perceived as distant and impractical, the God of the poor is not as effective as the God of the rich in giving life a purpose or in giving security in the face of death.

The middle class generally fits in between the rich (Class A) and the poor (Class D). The relative position of Class C in between Class B and Class D on many results indicates that both economic as well as educational status matter. However, it must be pointed out that Class C was often nearer to Class D than to Class B, suggesting the relatively stronger influence of education.

Findings about the more benevolent image of God and greater religiosity for the upper middle class cast doubt on the applicability of Western theories and findings about religion and social class for the Philippine situation. Both Marx and Weber predicted greater religiosity on the part of the poor. Their theories have, in fact, been corroborated by many observations of Western churches (see introduction of this chapter). A more orthodox faith and adherence to a code of conduct is supposedly characteristic of the exploited and submissive, whose faith legitimates for them the present order that keeps them in subjection and offers them compensation for their present deprivation by means of a promised afterlife. On the other hand, although religion serves the interest of the upper class and the upper middle class, it is implied that the ruling class is not truly religious. The ruling class supposedly sees through its own religion and practices it only to keep the essential faith alive in the lower class.[19] Such a contrived religiosity does not seem to apply to the upper-middle-class respondents in this study, as they were not just more frequent in their practices, but in their beliefs and feelings of closeness to God. In a study where anonymity was the rule, and where respondents were not even aware that social class was a variable, the upper middle class (especially the female sex) came across as a group in whose lives religion had genuine value and influence.

Why are the upper middle class in the Philippines more religious? Three possible interpretations, neither exhaustive nor mutually exclusive, could be advanced:

1. During the colonial past of the Philippines, the union of church and state dictated that God of the rich be closer to the established church. The *ilustrados* (intellectual and social elite) of the era mixed freely (at least more freely than the masses could) with the friars. The church was therefore identified with the rich, whether or not it was also an instrument to keep the masses submissive. Christianity was a social fact before it became a living faith. The rich therefore had more exposure to the official Catholic religion. Today the upper middle class continues to get more Catholic education through the exclusive Catholic schools. Although catechism is taught by volunteers in public schools, this structure does not have the same effect of integrating religion cognitively and affectively into so many young lives.
2. Religion, at least in the Philippines, could be seen by some as a higher order need. Maslow's hierarchy of needs starts with the basic physiological needs, such as the need for food and shelter. The urban poor have not satisfied this first rank in the hierarchy. This is not to deny the belief that a God-shaped vacuum exists in man or that it is impossible to keep one's faith alive amidst severe deprivation. The God-shaped vacuum, however, is more likely to show up when one has fulfilled basic needs and then wonders why, despite all this, something important still seems to be missing. Constant and active preoccupation with earning for the next meal is not conducive to reflection except in the most disciplined. The poor lack both the leisure and the intellectual abstraction to think about their faith.
3. Other things being equal, it is easier to be favorably disposed to one who has been good to you. Those who have been blessed have reason for gratitude. Associative conditioning imbues God, the reward giver, with the positive qualities that characterize life's rewards. The Fillipinos are a very grateful people; they have a strong sense of *utang na loob* (repaying a debt of gratitude). Only a very tenuous line, though, exists between gratitude and legitimation. What starts off as humble gratitude could lapse into a feeling of deservedness. One becomes extrareligious

out of gratitude and eventually one feels one is being rewarded for this religiosity. Eventually the two could be so blurred as to unwittingly produce an attitude such as that expressed by the Pharisee who prayed, "I thank God I am not like so and so." In this case, the rich could get so religiously self-righteous as to thank God that they are not like the irreligious poor! Such an attitude of legitimacy could serve to insulate the rich from confronting the problem of injustice.

On the other hand, it is also recognized that the poor might be closer to God because of their greater need for God, at least from a practical, worldly point of view. The poor need miracles, they need deliverance. Why then, do they not cling more closely to God? Perhaps a minimum experience of life's blessings is necessary for one to hope. Perhaps the poverty of the poor has been so consistent that they have not really tasted the goodness of God and, hence, do not expect him to be much different in the future. Thus, a state of learned hopelessness and helplessness results. Certainly one cannot conclude from this study that the submission and tolerance of the poor are brought about by visions of compensation in a glorious life.

If the poor were deficient in knowledge and possibly even creed, this might be somewhat expected. Religious workers have often believed that the poor, despite their lack of official church knowledge and conventional religious practices, are somehow closer to God and compensate with a variety of folk religious practices. Except for reading the *Pasyon* and wearing black/purple clothes during Lent, however, there are no other instances in which Class D heads the other class groups. On all total scores for various dimensions of religiosity, wherever a significant difference occurs it is always the poor that emerge less religious, and this difference is especially large in the "closeness-to-God" dimension.

Before concluding this chapter, a few points of caution should be raised. The first point concerns how representative is the Katipunan area from which all four social classes were derived. Further replication on a wider scale would render the findings more conclusive. The second point concerns the limitation of psychosocial measures, which may not tap more transcendent aspects of religiosity. Perhaps an inherent core of feeling that there must be a God because we are finite undercuts all social classes. Nevertheless, it should be borne in mind that this study does not conclude that urban poor Filipinos are not religious, but simply that they are less religious than the upper and middle classes, according to some conventional and common definitions of the word *religious,* and as ascertained from this particular survey.

Conclusion

To study the relationship between social class and religion, images of God, dimensions of religiosity, and locus-of-control orientations were explored in four social classes. It was found that the upper middle class consistently saw God as more benevolent, whereas the lower class was more likely to see God as powerful but detached. Social class status was also significantly and positively related to strength of belief in orthodox creed, to closeness to God, to frequency of seasonal religious practices, and to knowledge about religion. No consistent pattern was observed for locus-of-control (self versus God) orientation. Results were compared to Western findings and discussed in the light of Marx's and Weber's predictions.

NOTES

1. Unless specifically stated otherwise, the term *religion* is used in its general and commonly accepted sense as "a system of beliefs and practices pertaining to a deity."
2. Emile Durkheim, *The Elementary Forms of the Religious Life,* trans. Joseph Ward Swain (New York: Free Press, 1965), 62.
3. Mark 10:17–31; Matthew 19:16–30; Luke 18:18–25.
4. Max Weber, *The Protestant Ethic and the Spirit of Capitalism* (London: Allen & Unwin, 1930). First published in 1904.
5. Betty R. Scharf, *The Sociological Study of Religion* (London: Hutchinson & Company, 1970), 132–33.
6. K. Samuelsson, *Religion and Economic Action* (London: Heinemann, 1961).
7. Karl Marx and Friedrich Engels, *On Religion* (Moscow: Foreign Languages Publishing House, 1957).
8. Max Weber, *The Sociology of Religion* (London: Social Science Paperbacks, 1966). First published in 1922, Germany.

9. O. Maduro, *Religion and Social Conflicts,* trans. Robert R. Barr (New York: Orbis Books, 1979), xiii.
10. Susan Budd, *Sociologists and Religion* (London: Collier-MacMilland, 1973), 104.
11. Ibid.
12. Scharf, *The Sociological Study of Religion,* 83.
13. L. Ugalde, S. J., Foreward to Maduro, *Religion and Social Conflicts.*
14. John P. Robinson and Phillip R. Shaver, *Measures of Social Psychological Attitudes,* rev. ed. (Michigan: University of Michigan Institute for Social Research, 1973).
15. For all comparisons, the group with the higher frequency for that activity is mentioned first. When groups are put together, e.g., BCD, although they are ordered according to frequency, they are not significantly (statistically) different from one another.
16. Frank Lynch, S. J., and Perla Makil have important related findings in this matter in particular, and on social class and religion in general, in "The BRAC 1967 Filipino Family Survey," *Saint Louis Quarterly* 6 (1968):293–330.
17. Each locus-of-control item given here is *internal* in direction, i.e., it attributes control to oneself. In the questionnaire, the items were paired with statements that attributed control to God (external), e.g., "Sometimes I feel only God has control over the direction my life is taking."
18. Reynaldo Ileto, *Pasyon and Revolution: Popular Movements in the Philippines, 1840–1910* (Quezon City: Ateneo de Manila University Press, 1979).
19. Maduro, *Religion and Social Conflicts.*

10

The Biblical God from the Perspective of the Poor

JERRY ITUMELENG MOSALA

The emergence of liberation theology in Latin America and of black theology, feminist theology, and African theology in the United States and Africa, represents the unwillingness of the poor and oppressed people of the world to accept, as final, the definitions of Christian doctrines, not least the doctrine of God, emanating out of the context of the dominant classes of society. Although there is truth in the assertion that in every age the dominant ideas are the ideas of the dominant groups, there is equal validity in the view that nothing can stop the idea whose time has come. Within the framework of the business of *believing* among the politically and economically exploited people in the world, the impact of the history and experience of the poor on their faith represents an idea whose moment has arrived.

This chapter will attempt to show that God is as central to the faith of the poor as to the faith of the rich; but it will further seek to show that the God of the faith of the poor is not the same as the God of the faith of the rich. In point of fact, the two Gods stand in antithetical relationship to each other, reflecting the struggles between the rich and poor. If they did not, justice could not be a fundamental attribute of the God of the Bible as seen by poor people. The biblical God is mediated to the poor through a double process—of the historical experience of the poor of the Bible and the historical experience of the poor of today. Gustavo Gutierrez puts it aptly when he writes about these historical mediations: "Commitment to the process of liberation introduces Christians into a world quite unfamiliar to them and forces them to make what we have called a qualitative leap—the radical challenging of a social order and of its ideology and the breaking with old ways of knowing ('epistemological rupture')."[1]

Knowledge of God by the poor, therefore, is inextricably bound with their historical experiences as the poor. The importance of this for a Third World theological understanding of God cannot be overemphasized.

Who Are the Poor?

It is necessary to say a word about who the poor are because of the way in which the basic contradiction of our international economic system has caused many Christians to mystify, in theological terms, the reality of poverty. The scandal of our economic system is that the increased process of accumulation of material goods for the benefit of a few develops in equal proportion to the increased immiserization of the masses of people in the world. Few people possess and control more and more, whereas more and more possess and control less and less.

As this has become more evident, theologians have responded by mystifying the reality of poverty. It is being claimed that poverty should not be reduced to a lack of material goods. This is called "only one side" of the coin of poverty. The other side is what is called spiritual poverty, emanating out of too many possessions and therefore expressing itself as a feeling of meaninglessness in the midst of plenty.

This is to psychologize poverty and fail to see the brutal violence that is inherent in the condition of the poor. Further, it is to read the Bible with the comfortably tinted lenses of middle-class society. The biblical texts that are normally adduced in support of the spirituality of poverty are those that evolve directly out of the hermeneutical crisis produced by the tragedy of exile, in the case of the Old Testament, and those that issue out of the hermeneutical context of early Christianity in the slave-based economy of the Roman Empire.

There is, therefore, no fundamental distinction between material and "spiritual" poverty in the Bible. What we do have is the difference in the hermeneutical contexts of poverty. To understand this difference it is well to keep in mind what J. A. Sanders says about "hermeneutic modes":

> Behind whatever hermeneutic rules the biblical thinkers employed there were two basic modes: the constitutive and the prophetic, and both were valid. . . . At those historical moments when Israel was weak

and needed reconstituting, the Bible in its canonical shape seems to indicate that the constitutive mode was proper: our father Jacob was a wandering Aramean (Deut. 26:5); maybe like him we mark another beginning and not the end of Israel. But if that same mode of rereading of the tradition about Jacob, or Abraham, was read at a time when Israel had power, and had somehow confused it with God's power, then Jeremiah and Ezekiel, as well as the other prophets, called it false prophecy. . . . At that historical moment the prophetic mode is indicated: it may be we must wander, once more, like Jacob, long enough to rediscover our true identity.[2]

Who, then, are the poor? Gustavo Gutierrez paints a dramatic but accurate picture of poverty and the poor:

What we mean by material poverty is a subhuman situation. As we shall see later, the Bible also considers it this way. Concretely, to be poor means to die of hunger, to be illiterate, to be exploited by others, not to know that you are being exploited, not to know that you are a person. It is in relation to this poverty—material and cultural, collective and militant—that evangelical poverty will have to define itself.[3]

The poor are the products of a historical process of dispossession and expropriation. In certain circumstances this process is natural, being brought upon a people through such disasters as earthquakes, floods, cyclones, etc. Very often, however, the historical process of dispossession and expropriation is man-made. It is the result of socioeconomic systems based on inequity and exploitation. The Deuteronomistic writer of the Old Testament describes, in a passage that is conveniently ignored by scholars and Christians alike, in vivid dramatic terms, how the tributary exploitative social relations of the Israelite monarchy would bring into existence a subhuman class of poor people:

So Samuel told all the words of the Lord to the people who were asking a king from him. He said, "These will be the ways of the king who will reign over you: he will take your sons and appoint them to his chariots and to be his horsemen, and to run before his chariots; and he will appoint for himself commanders of fifties, and some to plough his ground and to reap his harvest and to make his implements of war and the equipments of his chariots. He will take your daughters to be perfumers and cooks and bakers. He will take the best of your fields and vineyards and olive orchards and give them to his servants. He will take your menservants and maidservants, and the best of your cattle and your asses, and put them to his work. He will take the tenth of your flocks, and you shall be his slaves. And in that day you will cry out because of your king, whom you have chosen for yourselves; but the Lord will not answer you in that day (1 Sam. 8:10ff. RSV).

This process of impoverishment had reached repugnant levels by the eighth century B.C.E. in Israel. As a result, the invectives of the prophets were directed against it:

> They covet fields, and seize them,
> and houses, and take them away;
> they oppress a man and his house
> a man and his inheritance (Mic. 2:2 RSV).
>
> I will not revoke the punishment;
> because they sell the righteous for silver
> and the needy for a pair of shoes—
> they that trample the head of the poor into the dust
> of the earth, and turn aside the way of the afflicted
> (Amos 2:6–7 RSV).

The historical process whereby a class of poor people is created is eloquently attested throughout the Bible. But perhaps the most impressive summary is the one given by the prophet Ezekiel:

> The leaders are like lions roaring over the animals they have killed. They kill the people, take all the money and property they can get, and by their murders leave many widows. The priests break my law and have no respect for what is holy. . . . The government officials are like wolves tearing apart the animals they have killed. They commit murder in order to get rich. The prophets have hidden these sins like men covering a wall with whitewash. . . . The wealthy cheat and rob. They ill-treat the poor and take advantage of foreigners (Ezek. 22:23ff. Good News Bible).

The history of the creation of the poor in the Third World, like the history of the poor in the Bible, is written in letters of blood and fire. The poor were first created through the process of colonization whose success depended on the existence of a landless class of former agriculturists and pastoralists. The process that E. P. Thompson describes aptly with respect to the creation of the poor in Britain is known to have been repeated with even greater brutality in the Third World. Thompson writes about Britain: "In agriculture the years between 1760 and 1820 are the years of wholesale enclosure, in which, in village after village, common rights are lost; and the landless and—in the south—pauperized labourer is left to support the tenant-farmer, the landowner, and the tithes of the Church. . . . In the mills and in many mining areas these are the years of the employment of children (and of women underground)."[4]

Describing the outcome of this process of dispossession, Colin Bundy paints an even dimmer picture with respect to the South African situation:

> There exists a vast and depressing body of evidence as to the nature and extent of underdevelopment in the Reserves (and particularly the Ciskei and Transkei) in the forty years that followed the 1913 (Land) Act: the details abound of infant mortality, malnutrition, diseases and debility, of social dislocation expressed in divorce, illegitimacy, prostitution and crime; of the erosion, desiccation and falling fertility of the soil; and of the ubiquity of indebtedness and material insufficiency of the meanest kind. The cumulative effect of these features is not easily described; life moulded by them was not lightly endured.[5]

In my country, as in many other Third World countries, the poor thus created were expected in the midst of their expropriation to believe that history, as it was happening to them, was consonant with the nature of the God of the Bible.

Having been dispossessed of their fundamental means of livelihood, the poor are kept poor from generation to generation through a process of creating a permanent "reserve army of labor," entry into and exit out of which is tightly controlled to ensure the continued existence of a class of poor, superexploitable people. Unemployment and poverty, at a time in history when technology has been developed to levels whereby all of mankind's needs can be met with relative ease, are not accidental. And the faith in and understanding of God of the poor of the world are hammered out of such a context.

The Biblical God in the Perspective of the Poor

It is only in the context of active resistance and struggle for social justice that there emerges a new encounter between the poor and God. In Latin America, as in other parts of the Third World, the poor begin to reappropriate the biblical God in their own ways as they start to identify kindred struggles in the very pages of Scripture. The old ways of reading Scripture become obsolete and new ways evolve. Gutierrez has this in mind when he writes: "In this context the theology of liberation arose. It could not have arisen before the populist movement and its historical praxis of liberation had reached a certain level of maturity. The struggles of the common people for liberation provide the matrix for a new life and a new faith, both to be achieved through a new kind of encounter with God and our fellow human beings."[6]

The most basic point that Gutierrez is making, and that this chapter is also advancing, is that the God of the poor is not predefined on the basis of certain metaphysical considerations. The poor are not given to metaphysics. That is the luxury of liberal and bourgeois theologians. On the contrary, the God of the poor, like the God of the Bible, is the fundamental *force* at the heart of history and is to be known and discovered only through a deliberate engagement in history.

This is the thread that runs through José M. Bonino's chapter, significantly entitled "Blessed Are the Doers," in his book *Christians and Marxists.*[7] Bonino starts this chapter by demonstrating that in the Bible to know God is to do justice. He shows how prophet after prophet in the Old Testament, and how the Gospel of John in the New Testament, attest to the fact that knowledge of God is knowledge of what God does in history to bring about justice. And then in a significant paragraph Bonino gives a biting criticism of the dominant modes of perceiving God: "Seen in the perspective of our dichotomising thought, this formulation (to do justice *is* to know God) smacks of an intolerable 'horizontalism'; it seems to be mere humanistic philanthropy, and naturally the interpreters try to supplement it with some 'religious' content. But what needs to be changed is not the Biblical formulation, but our perspective."[8]

For the poor of the world it is not necessary to change the biblical formulations. Their own contexts of social struggles enable them to see, without need for the harmonizations proposed by biblical critics, the true nature of the Bible as the product and the *site* of sociohistorical struggles. And their God, like the God of the Bible, is encountered in the crucible of these struggles. Historical engagement constitutes the theological epistemology of the poor. It is for this reason that the black South African migrant workers through the theology of the African independent churches have recaptured the social history of the precolonial societies as an epistemological tool by which to understand the biblical God in such a way that God is the supreme ancestor, while Christ is the *Nyanga* (Diviner). The metaphysical God and Christ of missionary theology would not do since they are extrahistorical. The full significance of the doctrine of God in African independent church theology has not yet been explored by Christian theologians, most probably because it is erroneously assumed by the latter that no developed doctrine of God can emerge among such an illiterate mass of marginal mortals as that which makes up the membership of these churches.

Thus black theology, in line with other theologies of liberation, and as the weapon of theory of the practical faith of oppressed and poor black people of the world, posits that to know who God is in the Bible and in the life of black Christians one must ask: what is the history of Israel and what is the history of black people? Without knowledge of the history of the Israelites there is no knowing the God of the Bible, and without knowledge of the history of black people there is no comprehending the God of poor black people.

That being the case, the assertion is valid for black theology that "when the world beyond the truth has disappeared, we shall establish the truth of this world."[9] If black theology is right in this, as we contend that it is, then we must acknowledge first that the truth of this world is that humanity is radically divided into a small class of rich and powerful people and a majority of poor and exploited people, the most exploited of the latter being black people and women. Second, and of greater importance for us *believers,* any doctrine of God that is not based on a historical engagement, which this reality calls for, is heretical and false prophecy.

This chapter would, however, be grossly misrepresentative of the biblical text if it created the impression that the God of the poor is the sole or even central actor in the pages of the Bible. There are other gods in the Bible, just as there are classes other than the poor. In fact, although Yahweh, the God of the poor, could not be suppressed in the biblical texts, this is not necessarily the dominant God of the Bible. The biblical text is as much an *arena* of fierce social struggles—with gods taking opposing sides—as our own lives today are *sites* of conflicts. So that it is patently clear that even as the name of Yahweh is used as an ideological justification for the state apparatuses of the Israelite monarchy during the times of David and

Solomon, other gods with completely different characters are meant.

Thus the onesidedness of this chapter in relation to the God of the poor is not a weakness, but a historical choice facing the poor of the world if they are to liberate the Bible so that the Bible can liberate them. It is a deliberate option for the one God among others in the Bible: Yahweh the God of justice. This option is a function of a hermeneutical class struggle in which the poor insist

> on a much more common-sensical and straightforward reading of what Jesus was saying and doing. When he speaks of emptying the prisons, they refuse to reduce this to "Spiritual prisons", since the cell blocks they and their friends and loved ones languish in are made of stone and steel. When he talks about cancelling debts, they think first of all not of infractions of social decorum but of their unpaid bills and the hot breath of their creditors. When he speaks of filling the hungry, they think not of communion wafers, but of rice and beans and bread: "Thy Kingdom . . . on earth."[10]

It must follow from this, therefore, that the poor neither know how nor have the propensity to talk of God ontologically. This is in line with the biblical God from whom they take their cue. Yahweh is the God who brings a people into being because Yahweh is the God of a people who bring themselves into being. The God of the poor is inseparable from the struggle of the poor for liberation. He/She precedes the poor because the poor precede him/her. He/She is both the cause and the product of a community struggling for a just society. He/She has no being apart from this community just as this community has no being apart from him/her.

Needless to say, the position advanced in this chapter must reveal that the God of the poor is different from the God of the rich, and that the gospel of Jesus Christ can only be properly proclaimed if this difference is recognized. Gone are the days when theologians and preachers declared like John Wesley that, notwithstanding the material differences between social classes, spiritually "there is at least equality of opportunity in sin and grace for rich and poor." What Thompson says about Wesleyan and Lutheran theology is particularly relevant for our understanding of the God of the poor: "And this reminds us that Lutheranism was also a religion of the poor; and that as Munzer proclaimed and as Luther learned to his cost, spiritual egalitarianism had a tendency to break its banks and flow into temporal channels, bringing thereby perpetual tension into Lutheran creeds which Methodism has reproduced."[11]

The poor are moving a step further. They are claiming that the God of the rich and powerful is under judgment from Yahweh, the biblical God of the poor:

The Sovereign Lord says, "People of Israel, go to the holy place in Bethel and sin, if you must! Go to Gilgal and sin with all your might! Go ahead and bring animals to be sacrificed morning after morning, and bring your tithes every third day. Go ahead to offer your bread in thanksgiving to God, and boast about the extra offerings you bring! This is the kind of thing you love to do" (Amos 4:4ff.).

NOTES

1. Gustavo Gutiérrez, "The Hope of Liberation," *Mission Trends*, no. 3, (New York: Paulist Press, 1976), 64.
2. J. A. Sanders, "Hermeneutics," *IDB*, supplementary volume, (New York: Abingdon, 1976), 405.
3. Gustavo Gutiérrez, *A Theology of Liberation* (London: SCM Press Ltd., 1974), 289.
4. E. P. Thompson, *The Making of the English Working Class* (Harmondsworth: Penguin Books, 1963), 217.
5. Colin Bundy, *The Rise and Fall of the South African Peasantry*, (London: Heinemann, 1979), 221.
6. Gustavo Gutiérrez, "Liberation Theology and Progressivist Theology," *The Emergent Gospel*, eds. S. Torres and V. Fabella (New York: Orbis, 1978), 240.
7. José M. Bonino, *Christians and Marxists* (London: Hodder and Stoughton, 1976), 29ff.
8. Ibid., 35.
9. Karl Marx and Friedrich Engels, *On Religion* (New York: Schocken Books, 1964), 42.
10. Harvey Cox, Foreword, in G. Pixley, *God's Kingdom* (New York: Orbis Books, 1981), VIII.
11. E. P. Thompson, *The Making of the English Working Class*, 399.

11

God's Cause for the Poor in Light of the Christian Tradition

HANS SCHWARZ

If it is true that capitalism is an offspring of Christianity and if it is true that God blesses his children with earthly goods, then God is not on the side of the poor, but on the side of the rich. If this is the case, then we will always have the poor with us as part of a system of natural—or dare we call it supernatural—selection. Yet when we listen to the biblical documents, such caricatures are hardly shared. Though the biblical texts provide no uniform approach to poverty, they quite often disclose a close relation between God and the poor. This is in contrast to Greek culture, in which one, of course, gave alms to the beggar but did not consider the poor as enjoying the special protection of the gods. In Israel, however, the protection of the innocent and of the socially weak was part of the order of life.

The Poor in the Israelite Tradition

The nomadic or seminomadic existence of the Israelite tribes prior to the settlement of the Promised Land was not characterized by a strict or entrenched distinction between rich and poor. All the Israelites enjoyed more or less the same standard of living since all had the same privileges and banded together to defend the community.

Things changed drastically once the full implications of a settled life became realized. At first each Israelite had his share of the Promised Land and property was zealously protected, as the story of Naboth and Ahab shows. When King Ahab wanted Naboth's vineyard, the latter replied: "The Lord forbid that I should give you the inheritance of my fathers" (1 Kings 21:3). Commerce and the buying and selling of property for profit were still unimportant factors in the Israelites' lives. Even excavations of the early period of

Israel (c. tenth century B.C.E.) show that all the houses were of the same size and arrangement.[1] Each house represents the dwelling of a family that lives in the same way as its neighbors. Though there were some exceptions to these middle-class standards (cf. Naboth or Job), even the first two kings of Israel (Saul and David) came from only moderately well-to-do families. The equality in the standard of living can be seen, for instance, at Tirsah near present-day Nablus, where the houses of the tenth century B.C.E. are all of the same size and arrangement.[2]

During the time of the monarchy, however, the economy was on the upswing and socioeconomic differentiations became more marked. The monarchical institutions produced a new class of officials who profited from their posts and from the favors granted them by the king. Those with real estate were alone entitled to be citizens and also functioned as judges. Some people made vast profits from their lands either through hard work or through luck. When we come to the eighth century B.C.E., the time of Amos, Micah, and Isaiah, the housing pattern at Tirsah is quite different. The rich houses are bigger and better built and are located in a different quarter from that where the houses of the poor are huddled together. This indicated that between these two centuries a social revolution had taken place, and we can understand why in the name of Yahweh the early prophets became the advocates of the poor against the mighty, rich, and powerful. This new situation is described by Hosea when we hear Ephraim (i.e., Israel) saying: "Ah, but I am rich, I have gained wealth for myself" (Hos. 12:8). But then this statement is immediately qualified: "But all his riches can never offset the guilt he has incurred." The new wealth is also indicated by Isaiah when he says: "Their land is filled with silver and gold, and there is no end to their chariots" (Isa. 2:7). The prophets do not admire the newly gained wealth; rather we hear: "Woe to those who join house to house, who add field to field, until there is no more room" (Isa. 5:8). The rich push the poor into a corner. "They covet fields and seize them; and houses, and take them away; they oppress a man and his house, a man and his inheritance" (Mic. 2:2). The rich landlords speculate and defraud others (Amos 8:5); the judges take bribes (Isa. 1:23), and the creditors know to pity (Amos 2:6–8).

Though the poor suffer from these injustices and are driven even more into destitution, they have two mighty advocates, Yahweh and his prophets. We hear that Yahweh will listen to the cries of those who are mistreated, for Yahweh is compassionate (Exod. 22:27). The poor even seem to be his special people and not the rich. So he tells the princes and the elders: "It is you who have devoured the vineyard, the spoil of the poor is in your houses. What do you mean by crushing my people, by grinding the face of the poor" (Isa. 3:14f.) Small wonder the eschatological hopes included the hope that "they shall sit every man under his vine and under his fig tree, and none shall make them afraid" (Mic. 4:4).

The Lord's promises are directed to the people as a whole. All are inheritors of the promised land. Thus we read in the Deuteronomic law: "A land in which you will eat bread without scarcity, in which you will lack nothing . . . and you shall eat and be full, and you shall bless the Lord your God for the good land he has given you" (Deut. 8:9f.). Of course, the Deuteronomic law is realistic that history cannot be turned back. "The poor will never cease out of the land" (Deut. 15:11). This, however, does not imply a status quo, since charity is not optional. "I command you," says the Lord: "You shall open wide your hand to your brother, to the needy and to the poor, in the land" (Deut. 15:11). But handouts, even if liberally given, do not change the social structure. Therefore, there were regulations designed to prevent poverty and to restore a certain equality between the Israelites: "At the end of every seven years you shall grant a release. And this is the manner of the release: every creditor shall release what he has lent to his neighbor; he shall not exact it of his neighbor, his brother, because the Lord's release has been proclaimed. Of a foreigner you may exact it; but whatever of yours is with your brother your hand shall release. But there will be no poor among you." (Deut. 15:1–4). This Sabbath year, which is introduced here, is quite different from the earlier Sabbath arrangement in Exodus 23:10f. and Leviticus 25:1ff. In Exodus we read: "For six years you shall sow your land and gather in its yield; but the seventh year you shall let it rest and lie fallow, that the poor of your people may eat; and what they leave the wild beasts may eat. You shall do likewise with your vineyard, and with your olive orchard" (Exod. 23:10f.).

We notice in both passages the social aspect of the divine commandment. Yet the underlying social structure of Exodus and Leviticus is agricultural or even a seminomadic existence. Perhaps, the sacred Sabbath for the land reflects an even earlier custom, still in use until fairly recently among seminomads. The fields were periodically redistributed by casting lots.[3] One can even assume that at each Sabbath year a new distribution of the fields occurred among those entitled to them within the tribe or the kinship.

In Deuteronomy we no longer hear that at every Sabbath year the produce of the lands should be left to the destitute. The first point that is made now is that a release from indebtedness shall be granted in each Sabbath year. Truly, the earlier regulation had also included provisions to remedy the inequities of the community arising through indebtedness or even slavery. But in Deuteronomy we encounter a situation that portrays such a differentiated society that it is impossible to start *de novo.* When we hear about a freeing of all indentured slaves and of the returning of the property every fifty years (Lev. 25:10), we wonder to what extent this was put into practice. Most likely it was much more idealistic thinking than actual reality. Even with the Deuteronomic sabbatical regulations one is hesitant to accord it with then current practice. There is certainly a tension between that kind of legislation and the reality to which the prophets point.

For example, we hear Yahweh say the following according to Ezekiel: "The people of the land have practised extortion and committed robbery; they have oppressed the poor and needy, and have extorted from the sojourner without redress. . . . Therefore I have poured out my indignation upon them; I have consumed them with the fire of my wrath, their way have I requited upon their heads" (Ezek. 22:29, 31).

This statement is remarkable on at least two accounts. First, as occurred similarly in the ancient Near East where the poor enjoyed the special protection of the gods, Yahweh here becomes the special advocate of the poor. In Psalm 82 Yahweh even accuses the other gods of showing partiality to the wicked and not maintaining the right of the afflicted and the destitute (Ps. 82:1ff.). Second, in Ezekiel the claim is made that the collapse of the Jewish state is due to the unjust social situation. God punishes the country because of its peoples' social crimes.

In some instance the terms *rich* and *poor* carry no moral or religious connotations. In contrast to the rich and influential elite, the poor are no separate social class. They are individuals, such as the fatherless children or the widows, and precisely in this social isolation they were defenseless. Occasionally, the thought is expressed that the pious and virtuous will prosper as God rewards them for their obedience to his law (cf. Ps. 112:1–3). Job is confronted with the corollary argument that he was not right with

God, otherwise he would not have been afflicted with so much evil and poverty. But he protests against the insinuation that there is a direct correlation between human righteousness and earthly prosperity. Wisdom literature picks up a different line of correlation when it shows that poverty is a consequence of a human activity or inactivity. The remarks that poverty stems from laziness (Prov. 6:11), seeking pleasure (Prov. 21:17), gluttony, and drunkenness (Prov. 23:21) do not excuse poverty or attempt to preserve the status quo. On the contrary, they are meant to prevent people from falling into poverty through wrong behavior. They do not condone the haughty behavior of the rich, but rather point to their moral obligation toward the poor.

There is another interesting line of reasoning in the Old Testament. God has a special preference for the small and weak to be his agents in history (cf. Judg. 6:15f.). He chooses the small and unimportant Israel to be his people. When they select their first king again, he points to someone small and insignificant whom no one else would have chosen. God delivers and exalts the humble and lonely and he brings down the haughty (Ps. 18:27). This does not just mean that he helps those who are economically poor, but also those who are downcast and who are in all kinds of misery. This is a special hope of liberation connected with the day of the Lord when all the proud and mighty are brought down and the Lord alone will be exalted on that day (cf. Isa. 2:2–22). The meek and the poor will rejoice "in those days," when they will be vindicated and all twisting of the law and all extortion of property will come to an end (Isa. 29:19–21).

When we consider the role of the servant of Yahweh in Deutero-Isaiah, we notice that in the place of the meek and lowly this servant was bruised and afflicted. He became the means of salvation as one who "has borne our griefs and carried our sorrows" (Isa. 53:4). There are here two important emphases: (1) someone, i.e., the Messiah, suffers for us in a substituting way so that we do not encounter the wrath of God as we deserve; and (2) because of his suffering, he will be exalted, "he shall see the fruit of the travail of his soul and be satisfied" (Isa. 53:11). This means, first, that the suffering of this earth is of such magnitude that it cannot be overcome by us. It is taken up into God, who overcomes it through a gracious intervention. It also means that the construction of a classless society, of a society of happy people, is a wishful dream. Even the pursuit of happiness usually occurs at the expense of someone else.

Yet the recognition of the depth of disparity among humans cannot leave us immobilized. It is interesting that in the intertestamental literature we hear, on the one hand, that there will be no poor in the coming eon. But we also hear of the abuses of the rich and how their behavior is totally unjustified. This means that future heavenly justice does not serve as a way of postponing the need for necessary present-day justice. This is also the line of thought we will find in the New Testament.

The Poor in the New Testament

When we come to the New Testament we encounter to some extent a continuation of the Old Testament attitude toward rich and poor. According to Mark, Jesus observes that the scribes "devour widows' houses" (Mark 12:40), a situation that stands in analogy to the behavior of the mighty of the Old Testament. We also hear Jesus quote Deuteronomy 15:11, saying: "You always have the poor with you" (Mark 14:7). Then, however, he continues: "but you will not always have me."

Jesus' presence relativizes such important things as giving alms. This does not mean, however, that giving alms is an adiaphoron. Quite to the contrary, Jesus shows in the story of the widows' mite, that it is not sufficient simply to give large sums if we are rich. Jesus demands our total allegiance. In the dialogue with the rich ruler we hear Jesus mention the same point: "One thing you still lack. Sell all that you have and distribute to the poor, and you will have treasure in heaven; and come, follow me" (Luke 18:22). The allegiance to Jesus excludes any attachment to the riches of this world. Consequently, we hear Jesus say: "It is easier for a camel to go through the eye of a needle than for a rich man to enter the kingdom of God" (Luke 18:25).

The advantage of the poor is not that they are closer to the heart of God, but that they have nothing to be proud of and nothing to rely upon except God himself. The presupposition is that the poor can do nothing for themselves. They can only accept the unconditional grace of God. Of course, this approach would be contrary to any developmental policy in terms of self-help. Yet as finite beings humans are always dependent. The question is whether they rely on something that can be eaten by rust and moths or whether it is of enduring and infinite quality. Thus we also hear in Luke that Jesus asks to invite the poor, the maimed, the lame, and the blind to the banquet. They will accept the invitation, whereas the affluent have so many distractions that they find one excuse after another for not accepting the eschatological invitation (cf. Luke 14:12–24).

Especially Luke emphasizes Jesus' attention to the poor and the disadvantaged. For instance, he relates Jesus' parable of the rich man and Lazarus (Luke 16:19–31), indicating that earthly prosperity does not necessitate eternal rewards, and the poor may indeed inherit eternal bliss. It is interesting that in this parable we do not hear of any merit of the poor or any explicit criticism of the rich. Almost by necessity riches separate one from the kingdom of God even if there are no explicit transgressions against God's will. The hope of the poor, however, is directed toward the hereafter, since it appears the affairs of this world will always be characterized by injustice and greed. Only through confrontation with the gospel is there a change of heart and mind possible for the rich. Once the rich chief tax collector Zacchaeus realized that he was accepted by God, he responded: "Behold, Lord, the half of my goods I give to the poor; and if I have defrauded any one of anything, I restore it fourfold" (Luke 19:8). Small wonder that Jesus reacts to such change with the good news: "Today salvation has come to this house" (Luke 19:9).

Universal brotherhood and sisterhood and equality in rank and possession are not human possibilities. We have seen too often how revolutionary slogans of equality have bred new atrocities and exploitation whether of the Eastern socialist kind or of the Western middle-class breed. As Karl Marx advocated, revolutions indeed bring into history an eschatological hope. Since they cannot realize what they promise, however, they are actually projections of one's dreams into the foreseeable future. In the story of Zacchaeus, however, we encounter the redundant anticipation of the eschatological goal made possible through the experience with the gospel and its embodiment in Jesus of Nazareth. This corresponds to Jesus' own understanding of his ministry.

At the first sermon in his hometown, Nazareth, he quotes the messianic announcement of the nearness of God according to Isaiah 61:1f.: "The Spirit of the Lord is upon me, because he has annointed me to preach good news to the poor. He has sent me to proclaim release to the captives and recovering of sight to the blind, to set at liberty those who are oppressed, to proclaim the acceptable year of the Lord" (Luke 4:18f.).

Poverty is here brought into the broader context of all of those who are on the underside of the world. To those the Messiah will preach the good news that their lot will be changed. Jesus comments on this passage: "Today this scripture has been fulfilled in your hearing" (Luke 4:21). In a similar way he responds to John the Baptist's inquiry whether Jesus is the Messiah or whether he should wait for another one by telling John's disciples: "Go and tell John what you have seen and heard, the blind receive their sight, the lame walk, lepers are cleansed, and the deaf hear, the dead are raised up, the poor have good news preached to them. And blessed is he who takes no offense at me" (Luke 7:22f.). In the same direction go the beatitudes in which we read according to Luke "Blessed are you poor" (Luke 6:20) instead of the Matthean: "Blessed are the poor in spirit" (Matt. 5:3).

The one who had nowhere to lay his head (Matt. 8:20) demanded in a radical way that those who followed him be oblivious to earthly goods. But Jesus neither advocated squandering these goods nor was he an ascetic like John the Baptist. Pious circles even called him a glutton and a drunkard, a friend of tax collectors and sinners, i.e., of rich people (Matt. 11:19). By no means were all his followers poverty stricken, nor did they become so once they joined him. In the parable of the workers in the vineyard he lets the owner answer: "Am I not allowed to do what I choose with what belongs to me" (Matt. 20:15)? This is not to be misunderstood in the often claimed fashion that possessions do not call for social responsibility. On the contrary, as the parable shows there should be no begrudging of liberal giving.

Jesus does not stage a social protest in the face of the immense socioeconomic injustices of his time. He demonstrates what the will of God demands—not clinging to our goods, but sharing them with others. This is even more necessary in the face of the approaching kingdom. Why should we heap riches in this world and thereby lose our soul (cf. Luke 12:20)? It is important that all our hope and trust is centered in God and his grace instead of anything we might be able to do to secure our future. At the same time, the future is not completely outstanding. The "follow me" implies a different style of life and a different allegiance than to be found in this world. It is not just following the example Jesus set in his life; it also implies that through contact with the Divine a new attitude is indeed possible. Jesus does not just set an example, but through his own person enables us to follow him. This becomes especially clear once we come to Paul and the nascent Christian community.

Paul tirelessly emphasizes that with Jesus something new has occurred, and that through our accepting Jesus' salvific benefits we are indeed new persons. So we hear his conclusions drawn from one baptism: "We were buried therefore with him [i.e., Christ Jesus] by baptism into death, so that as Christ was raised from the dead by the glory of the Father, we too might walk in newness of life" (Rom. 6:4).

The new situation in which the first Christians found themselves and also the problems it involved is best portrayed in the so-called early Christian communism of love. When it is mentioned in Acts 2:44 and 4:32 that "they had everything in common," we see analogies in Aristotle's claim that "common is the property of friends."[4] The communal living that is envisioned, or rather reflected upon, in Acts is not only derived from the sense of belonging together. The neo-Marxist Ernst Bloch, in his *Principle Hope* (Prinzip Hoffnung), caught the motivation of the early Christian community correctly when he claimed that the expectation of the imminent end made them oblivious to the earthly provision for the future.[5] He also noticed that in the communal life-style the memory was reflected of Jesus' own life among his disciples and his exhortation not to be tied to the demands of the day. Thus "they devoted themselves to the apostles' teaching and fellowship, to the breaking of bread and prayers" (Acts 2:42). This charismatic, enthusiastic community did not worry about property or the future. Important items were only faithfulness to Jesus as the Christ and the missionary proclamation of the gospel among the Jewish community. Everything connected with this eon became secondary.

As the community rapidly increased in size, it became more and more difficult to distribute the goods fairly among all members (Acts 6:1ff.). When there arose a famine under Emperor Claudius (Acts 11:29), Paul and Barnabas collected money for the suffering Christians in Jerusalem and the surrounding Judea. When Paul mentioned the poor among the saints in Jerusalem, for whom he was soliciting contributions, he did not only call them that way because this was a title of honor, but certainly because of their economic plight. As the enthusiastic expectations of an immediate return of the Lord faded and the mission expanded to the ends of the then known world, such communal life-style was simply impractical because it did not gainfully procure for the future. To counteract these enthusiastic tendencies Paul tells the Christians at Thessalonica to work with their hands so that they would command the respect of outsiders and depend on nobody (1 Thess. 4:11f.). In another letter to the same congregation he even warns: "If anyone will not work, let him not eat" (2 Thess. 3:10), a caution that made it into the Russian constitution.[6] Paul himself made sure that he was not a burden to anybody and supported himself on his journeys by making tents (Acts 18:3).

Since Christians came from all walks of life, there were socioeconomic distinctions between individual members. This is especially noticeable in Corinth, where at the Lord's Supper these discrepancies between rich and poor were even more pronounced (1 Cor. 11:21). Paul indicated with his admonitions that they still have to learn social responsibility, since unlike Hellenistic religions the barriers of class are secondary among Christians. On the one hand Paul can say with the Jerusalem enthusiasts: "The appointed time has grown very short" (1 Cor. 7:29). Therefore all allegiances to this world, its goods, and concerns are unimportant. But on the other hand, he can also argue for equality among Christians from a different basis. Since Christians have put off their old nature with its practices and put on the new nature, "there cannot be Greek and Jew, circumcised and uncircumcised, barbarian, Scythian, slave, free men, but Christ is all, and in all" (Col. 3:9ff.).

There is a new community emerging in which the old barriers of class and social rank, which were thought to be unchangeable, are suddenly declared nonexistent. But since "the Lord is at hand" (Phil. 4:5), it is a waste of time to change these distinctions. One should not worry about them, since soon the barriers will collapse anyway. It does not make sense to abolish slavery or dispose of amassed riches. "In whatever state each was called, there let him remain with God" (1 Cor. 7:24). In faith, however, these separating barriers are overcome, since all are one in Christ. When they gradually modified the enthusiasm about the imminent Parousia, the Christians did not endow the status quo of rank and status with permanence. On the contrary, the newly won equality in faith contained immense social dynamism. Once the notion was commonly accepted that the Parousia was not as imminent as many had first thought, their equality in faith sought ways in which it could be incarnated.

It is interesting that Friedrich Engels observed that in the name of the Judeo-Christian tradition actual societal changes take place, whereas in other societies reform movements "are clothed in religion but they have their source in economic causes; and yet, even when they are victorious, they allow the old economic conditions to persist untouched."[7] But for the Christians the temptation was great to leave unchanged the economic conditions in which they found themselves. Not without reason the letter of James warns that the pattern of rich and poor prevailing in the world shall not be continued in the Christian community (James. 2:2–4). The flame of a new kind of hope and of a new orientation in life could not be extinguished. Though compromised a thousand times, it continued to offer its transforming power.

Poverty and the Care for the Poor in the Christian Church

In the Greco-Roman world there were many social support systems. Bread and games was a popular cry in ancient Rome, and philanthropy was not unknown in ancient Greece. Though often the poor benefited most from these measures, neither the Greeks nor the Romans felt a religious, moral, or governmental obligation to help the poor. As we have seen, this was different in the Judeo-Christian tradition. The Christian *koinonia* (Acts 2:42) necessitated a caring for each other. The remark of the pagans that Christians love each other (related to us by Tertullian) was so revolutionary that it eventually changed the whole globe. Gerhard Uhlhorn summarized well this countercultural approach of the nascent church: "It was when the misery became greater and greater in the perishing world, when the arm of the state was more and more paralyzed, when the authorities no longer offered assistance to the poor and the oppressed, nay, themselves took a part in oppressing and exhausting them, that the church became on a grand scale the refuge of all the oppressed and suffering."[8]

Very early there were signs of institutionalization of the care for the poor. For instance, in the *agape* feasts needy people were given care packages, which they could take home to their families. Then there was the new office and status of the widows. In the face of the miserable economic situation and the social disadvantage of the widows in the lower classes, the office of the widows (cf. 1 Tim. 5:3–16) assumed great significance. It removed them from being mere recipients of alms and put them into a respectable position. Moreover, at the conclusion of the Sunday services alms were deposited before the presider, i.e., bishop, and then distributed by him to those who were in need. Naturally, the social responsibility of the nascent church was confined to its own members. Once the church grew, certain principles were necessary concerning which alms ought to be received and which not. One rejected, for instance, contributions from people who had amassed a fortune illegally or immorally.[9] The bishop's house had special storage facilities for the gifts that were to be distributed. Yet the church did not simply give handouts. Whereas the state gave to the habitually unemployed, the church tried to provide jobs for Christians without work or for those who had to forfeit their former employment because of their newfound faith. The understanding was that whoever could work should do so, and those who could not provide for themselves should be supported. This means that, in contrast to secular communities, there were no beggars in the Christian community. One also cared for the sick and visited them.

Yet it was not until the Constantinian era that the care for the poor became a comprehensive humanitarian enterprise. Up until then it had been simply an expression of Christian solidarity. This changed when the church became a majority religion. Now the church felt it had an obligation to the whole of society. This was promoted through the state, when, for instance, Constantine "issued supplies of food for the support of the poor, of orphan children, and widows."[10] Emperor Constantine himself felt that it was his special duty to care for the poor, a trait that certainly shows Christian influence.[11] The church could now also receive inheritances, which it could use for the care of the poor.

Basil the Great tackled the plight of the poor in word and deed. He suggested that from each inheritance a portion should be given to the poor. He also built a settlement for the poor outside Caesarea that was designed to house the sick, lepers, the poor, and strangers; it also served as a place to provide work for those who could still care for themselves. It was run with the support of the state. Gregory Nazianzen rightly said of Basil: "Basil's care was for the sick, and the relief of their wounds, and the imitation of Christ, by cleaning leprosy, not by a word, but in deed."[12] Many other places like this were created and in part had been established earlier. The care for the poor in special institutions was promulgated especially through monastic orders as they attached dwellings for the poor to monasteries, staffed these places with monks, and maintained them through the products of their work and through donations. Many well-off Christians displayed to posterity through inscriptions on their tombstones what kind of charitable enterprises they had supported.

Since in the Middle Ages times were often politically unstable, the earlier notion that church property was to be used for the poor and that the church should be an advocate of the poor was difficult to carry out. Even Charlemagne, who vigorously attempted to tackle the plight of the poor, was hardly successful. Although the Franks felt that tithing was voluntary, Charlemagne considered it mandatory since one-third of the tithes was set aside for the support of the poor. He also demanded that the affluent be additionally taxed to support the poor. Charlemagne attempted to settle the lot of the poor once and for all. But the vast dioceses were difficult to manage in an effort to support the poor, and the people did not cooperate either. Consequently, alms remained the main source for the support of the poor.

With the growth of urban life support for the poor was considered more and more a duty of the citizens, who established hospitals and other housing for the sick, the poor, and orphans. Since aiding the poor was considered a Christian virtue, citizens gave liberally. But often one did not inquire whether such help was for an emergency or for convenience. One also did not feel that it was a duty to help in such a way that the poor could leave the circle of poverty. God had put people in different classes and since the poor were in their place according to God's will, they should remain there. Giving alms was considered a good work and it was more important that one did good works than to consider what they effected. This sentiment changed drastically with the Reformation.

Martin Luther argued that there was no merit involved in helping the poor, rather it was a Christian duty. In his treatise *To the Christian Nobility,* he claimed that since Israel could eradicate begging, Christians should be able to do so too. He rejected an individualistic approach to solving poverty and demanded that each city should start caring for the poor by first abolishing begging. In many cities a common treasury was instituted to support the poor. Instead of public collections from house to house, offerings were taken up in church following proper admonition from the pulpit. Upon a trip to the Upper Rhine Valley in the summer of 1526, Gerhard Geldenhauer relates the following about the results of this new approach: "I was in Strassburg for a few days and saw the picture and the morals of a city which differs by far from other cities in which I was. There nobody begs, poor travellers are maintained by public means for one day and one night. When one is not sick one receives bread as a little something for the road and has to continue travelling. According to their circumstances poor citizens receive enough to be able to live honorably. All this is given in faith from public means." Geldenhauer further reports that swearing, oaths, unchastity, drunkenness, and gambling were outlawed under penalty of severe punishment through decrees by the city council.[13]

The Reformation brought a new view of poverty as something to be abolished. But it was not until the very recent democratization process of society that the state recognized its responsibility for the protection of both the individual citizen and of all groups in society in their desire for social security. Now it is gradually being recognized that mere handouts are insufficient not only because they perpetuate the status quo but because they infringe on the dignity and self-worth of the individual. In most countries social legislation has been introduced by establishing protective measures in favor of the helpless of society in the form of minimum wages, security measures at the working place, child labor regulations, social security, Medicaid and Medicare, to name just a few. Only a small amount of revenue still goes to work in what was traditionally perceived as the giving of alms; most of the money is applied toward protective and preventive measures.

The same change in help is true for the church's own work. The so-called social services programs provide only in a small measure direct charity, such as food or shelter. The major portion of the budget is used to assist individuals or groups in rejoining the mainstream of society and making them aware that, as children of God, all should share in God's bounty. The rediscovery that there is neither Greek nor Jew, neither slave nor free, and that the whole of society forms a community under the protective hand of God has led beyond a concern limited to one's own level in society; it has led theologians to call for "liberation from every form of exploitation, the possibility of a more human and more dignified life, the creation of a new man."[14]

There are signs in many other quarters too that indicate the poor of the world are not forgotten. There are many forms of developmental aid for younger countries and disaster relief funds in case of immediate need. Also, the United Nations is at least a forum where people from all nations can convene and express common concerns and desires. But one of the most pressing contemporary problems is still the great gulf between rich and poor within societies and also between different political states. When one considers the roughly three millennia of the Judeo-Christian tradition and the still existing discrepancy between rich and poor, one wonders whether any impact—not to mention progress—has been made.

God may well care for the poor, but his human agents do not seem to do so. If one thinks in this way, and there are many reasons why one could, there are few things that dare not be overlooked. The Christian church may not always have done a good job and it may often have been guided by wrong motives, but it has always felt a religious duty to help the poor. The example Jesus set and the practical consequences Paul drew on the basis of the Christ event have never been totally forgotten. Although it is fashionable in some quarters today to talk about the post-Christian era, the concern for the poor on a communal, societal, and global level cannot be sufficiently explained without pointing to the stimulus of the Judeo-Christian tradition. Even today it is one of the prime tasks of the church to sharpen the conscience of society.

In times of presumed affluence the church was often tempted to establish itself solidly in this world. But today it rediscovers more and more its servant role, pointing to a new future and modeling itself on the likeness of its Lord. It points to human solidarity and attempts to give a more human face to a cruel and competitive world through programs such as Church World Service, Caritas, Miserior, and Bread for the World. As it realizes that its presence in the world is challenged by ideologies from the Left and the Right and that it cannot take for granted its past privileges, it also rediscovers that one cannot identify with the poor unless one becomes one of them in spirit and action. As Christian base communities resembling those of the nascent church spring up in many younger countries, there is hope that one day the modern pagans will discover again that Christians love each other. They might even experience that they live more humanly if they let themselves be drawn into that love.

NOTES

1. Cf. Roland de Vaux, *Ancient Israel,* vol. 1: *Social Institutions* (New York:MacGraw-Hill, 1965), 72f.

2. Ibid., 72.

3. Hans-Joachim Kraus, *Gottesdienst in Israel. Grundriss einer alttestamentlichen Kultgeschichte* (Munich: Chr. Kaiser, 1962), 91.
4. Aristotle, *Niccomachian Ethics* 1968b.
5. Cf. Ernst Bloch, *Das Prinzip Hoffnung* (Frankfurt/Main: Suhrkamp, 1959), 3:1488.
6. Martin Hengel, *Eigentum und Reichtum in der frühen Kirche. Aspekte einer frühkirchlichen Sozialgeschichte* (Stuttgart: Calwer Verlag, 1973), 43.
7. Friedrich Engels, "On the History of Early Christianity" (1894/95), in Karl Marx and Friedrich Engels, *On Religion,* intr. by Reinhold Niebuhr (New York: Schocken, 1964), 317f., in a footnote by Engels.
8. Gerhard Uhlhorn, *Christian Charity in the Ancient Church* (New York: Scribner's, 1883), 362.
9. Cf. for details *Constitutions of the Holy Apostles* (4:3ff.) in Ante-Nicene Fathers 7:433f.
10. Eusebius, *The Life of Constantine* (4:28), in Nicene and Post Nicene Fathers of the Christian Church 1:547.
11. Ibid. (1:48), 1:494.
12. Gregory Nanzianzen, *The Panegyricon S. Basil,* Oratio 43:63, in Nicene and Post Nicene Fathers of the Christian Church 7:416.
13. According to Robert Stupperich, "Armenfürsorge IV," in Theologische Realenzyklopädie 4:31.
14. Gustavo Gutiérrez, *A Theology of Liberation,* trans. and ed. by C. Inda and J. Eagleson (Maryknoll, New York: Orbis, 1973), 306.

12

The God of the Oppressed and the God Who Is Empty*

JAY B. McDANIEL

To date, John May tells us, the Christian-Buddhist dialogue "has consisted mainly in exchanges between a small coterie of enthusiasts in Europe and Japan."[1] Among such enthusiasts we might list notable European-born Christian thinkers such as Ninian Smart, J. J. Spae, Hans Waldenfels, and William Johnston, plus Japanese Buddhist thinkers such as Keiji Nishitani, Shin'ichi Hisamatsu, and Masao Abe. All have made important contributions to cross-cultural interchange, and from their insights there is much to be learned. Nevertheless, as the somewhat critical tone of May's comments suggests, there has been no small trace of parochialism in some of the discussions to date. "If Christian-Buddhist dialogue is to take root and survive," May tells us, "it cannot afford to remain confined to discussions among an intellectual elite as it often has in Europe."[2] It must evolve beyond the preoccupations of a religious and philosophical elite toward an inclusion of the interests of the poor.

There is truth in May's point. For the past several decades, the dialogue between Buddhism and Christianity has been understood primarily as an interchange between East and West, and implicit in this understanding has been the assumption that Christian theology is *Western* theology. This supposition has indeed been valid for almost twenty centuries, with the important exception of Eastern Orthodoxy. In recent decades, however, a new tradition has been emerging within Christianity: one that considers itself biblically based, yet neither Eastern nor Western, given traditional meanings of the terms. This tradition is called liberation theology or, in some of its European and American versions, political theology.[3] It represents the experience of Christians who, given geopolitical and cultural meanings of East and West, arise out of, or speak in explicit solidarity with, the South. Specifically speaking, the word *South* can refer to the economically deprived and politically oppressed of the

Third World. More generally, it can refer to the materially destitute and socially disenfranchised of the entire world, including those who are victimized in the Third World, but not excluding those who similarly suffer in the First and Second Worlds. In the past, the dialogue between Christianity and Buddhism has not often included voices from this global South. In the present and foreseeable future, it is perhaps time for a change.

This change has been prefigured by Southeast Asian theologians such as Pierris, Balasuriya, and de Silva, who have been developing liberation perspectives within the context of an encounter with Buddhism. Another form of Christian theology that might facilitate this dialogue between Eastern Buddhism and the Christian South is process, or Whiteheadian, theology. Process thinkers such as John Cobb have been active in dialogues with Buddhists, and at the same time they have been developing political theologies of their own.[4] Indeed, taking clues from Cobb's writings on social and political issues on the one hand, and Buddhism on the other, it becomes evident that process thought may provide a paradigm by which to affirm, and yet not confuse, "the God of the oppressed" of whom liberation theologians speak and the ultimate reality of "emptiness" of which Mahayana Buddhists speak. Process theology may provide a bridge between the East and the South.

The purpose of this chapter is to explain and explore that possibility. It is to indicate a new direction that the Buddhist-Christian dialogue might take as liberation and political thinkers enter discussions. At best, this new direction would provide an occasion for growth in all participants involved: Buddhist and Christian, Eastern and Western, southern and northern, liberation-oriented and otherwise. My focus will be on the way liberation-oriented Christians—that is, those who speak either from, or in explicit solidarity with, the South—might be transformed as they encounter Buddhism. This focus reflects my own life situation—or, perhaps my own life dilemma—which is that of a Christian impressed by the truth of liberation points of view and yet simultaneously impressed by the truths of Buddhism.

The chapter is divided into five sections. In the first I explain the general distinction between emptiness and God as understood from a process perspective. In the second I discuss the God of the oppressed. In the third I discuss the God who is empty. In the fourth I explain why it might be desirable from a liberation perspective to appropriate the idea that God is empty. And in the fifth I explore the nature of a Christian faith that has been transformed through such appropriation.

Two Ultimates

It is sometimes assumed that the appropriate aim of dialogue between Christians and Buddhists is an identification of similar concerns. At the end of dialogue, so it is hoped, participants will understand that they have been concerned with the same realities despite verbal appearances to the contrary, and that their two traditions point to the same end. They will realize, as the saying goes, that the truth is one while the paths are many.

Contrary to expectations, the reality of dialogue often leads in a different direction. The more some Christians talk with Buddhists, and some Buddhists with Christians, the more it can seem to each that the truths themselves may be many. Discussions between Masao Abe and John Cobb provide a good illustration.

Both agree that the ultimates of their two traditions—emptiness for the Buddhist, and God for the Christian—are different.[5] Yet precisely amidst the recognition of such differences an interesting possibility emerges. If Abe, representing the Kyoto School of Japanese Buddhist thought, is right to affirm the ultimacy of transpersonal and nonteleological emptiness; and if Cobb, representing the process tradition of Christian thought, is right to affirm the ultimacy of a personal teleological God; then there may indeed be two truths: two ultimates to which their respective paths lead. It is not as if Buddhists must be wrong about emptiness if Christians are right about God, or that Christians must be wrong about God if Buddhists are right about emptiness. Perhaps both are right.

In fact this is what Cobb suggests. He suggests that both emptiness and God are real, though neither in a substantialist sense, and that each is ultimate in different respects. Emptiness is the ultimate reality of the cosmos: that universal and yet nonsubstantial activity, itself expressed as *pratitya samutpada,* of which all sentient beings, God included, are expressions. God is the ultimate actuality of the cosmos: that supremely sentient being by whom all other actualities can be drawn into the fullness of life, and in whose ongoing experience they are continuously gathered together. In the past, so Cobb suggests, Christianity (with the exception of apophatic mystical traditions) has usually stressed faith in God; whereas Buddhism (with the exception of Pure Land traditions) has usually stressed awakening to emptiness. The two religions have focused on ultimates that are real and yet different. In the future, Cobb proposes, participants in each tradition might thematize both.

As a process theologian, Cobb's proposal is heavily influenced by Whitehead. He draws upon Whitehead's distinction between creativity, as the ultimate activity of which all actualities are manifestations, and God, as a particular and yet primordial manifestation of this creativity. He is suggesting that Buddhist emptiness is analogous to Whitehead's creativity, and that the Christian God is analogous to Whitehead's conception of deity.[6] Yet Cobb's proposal is also influenced by the Western biblical heritage. Cobb rightly recognizes that the God of the Bible, like the God of Whitehead, is "a" being, indeed the supreme being, rather than "being itself." The medieval, scholastic identification of God with *esse ipsum,* or pure being, was a Greek-influenced revision and partial distortion of the biblical way of thinking. Except in certain styles of apophatic mysticism, the revision did not grasp the imagination of historical Christianity at the level of lived experience. Most Christians in the past and present have thought of God in biblical rather than mystical terms: as "a" being who is aware of the world, who cares for it, and who can guide living beings toward wholeness in this life and the next.

This biblical image has become increasingly important in world Christianity for those who speak from, or in solidarity with, the South. It strikes a resonant chord with those Christians in the First and Third Worlds who are victimized by, or concerned with, social injustices, and who see the Christian gospel as good news for the poor and oppressed. Drawing as they do from the prophetic traditions in the Bible, politically oriented theologians such as James Cone, Gustavo Gutiérrez, José Miguez-Bonino, Johann Baptist Metz, José Miranda, Jurgen Moltmann, Rosemary Ruether, Letty Russell, Dorothee Soelle, and Juan Luis Segundo do not think of God as a transpersonal and nonteleological ground analogous to pure being or pure nothingness. Instead, in instances where they speak of God, a personal being, analogous to the biblical Yahweh, who calls the world toward freedom and justice is meant. Cobb's suggestion that God is "a" being with character and form is partially motivated by his own desire to be faithful to the biblical heritage from which the insights of the above-mentioned individuals often stem. The God of Whitehead, so he argues, is analogous to the God of the Bible: a creator, not out of nothing as Greek-influenced

Christianity has so often insisted, but rather out of chaos.[7] And this God, as disclosed in the Exodus events and the preaching of Jesus, brings order out of chaos by availing possibilities for liberation.

Yet Cobb's distinction between emptiness and God is not motivated only by a desire to be faithful to the prophetic heritage of the Bible and to political theology. It is also motivated by a desire to be faithful to Buddhism. Cobb recognizes that the emptiness of which Masao Abe and other members of the Kyoto School speak, and of which many Buddhists throughout the ages have spoken, is misunderstood and misrepresented when equated with the biblical God. The truth of emptiness is lost when emptiness-as-such, itself neither good nor evil, is teleologized and therefore Christianized. If one looks within traditional Buddhism for any analogy to a biblical understanding of God, one must turn, not to traditional and contemporary discussions of emptiness, but rather to the Pure Land heritage and to the idea of Amida. As a cosmic Bodhisattva who vows to save all sentient beings, Amida, not emptiness, is the best analogy to the biblical God. Yet within Buddhism itself Amida is distinguished from emptiness. Amida is the Sambhogakaya, to be distinguished from emptiness, which is the Dharmakaya. This Sambhogakaya, or body of bliss, is the primordial form or manifestation of emptiness, just as in Whitehead God is the primordial form or manifestation of creativity. Cobb's proposal that emptiness and God are real and yet different is intended to be true to Buddhism even as it is true to biblical perspectives.

Whether Cobb's proposal can be accepted and internalized by Buddhists remains to be seen. The seeds for such internalization may already lie in Pure Land Buddhism, with its long tradition of openness to Amida. In the future it is possible that the Pure Land heritage can appropriate certain aspects of the biblical worldview, interpreting those aspects as further revelations of the nature of Amida. A Christianized Buddhism might even emerge, in which Pure Land Buddhists adopt the history of the ancient Near East, including that of biblical Christianity, as part of that universal history in which the vow of Amida has been disclosed.[8]

What is also clear, of course, is that Cobb's proposal opens the door for a Buddhized Christianity. Even as Pure Land Buddhists might learn from the biblical heritage, followers of the biblical heritage might learn from Buddhism. On the one hand, they might learn more about Yahweh through a study of Amida. There may be themes within Pure Land Buddhism that can supplement, complement, or transform biblical understandings of God. On the other hand, they might learn about emptiness. It is on this possibility that I focus. What would it mean for a biblically oriented Christian, perhaps one who is heavily influenced by liberation theology, to be open to a God who is empty? Again, a process perspective will be helpful.

The God of the Oppressed

The God to whom much southern Christianity points is, in the phrase of James Cone, a "God of the oppressed." The phrase means at least two things.[9] It means that God shares in the suffering of the poor and oppressed prior to their liberation, and it means that God is involved in their struggle to be liberated. The liberation at issue is not simply inward or spiritual liberation. It is not merely a liberation of the soul from worldly travail. Rather it is social liberation: a liberation of human lives from economic inequality and political repression for equality and freedom. The God to whom theologians such as Cone point is one who is involved in the struggle of the destitute for food, clothing, and shelter, who is engaged in the struggle of the disenfranchised for self-determination, a sense of dignity, and political power. This God is one who is pained by inequality and enslavement, and who is immersed in the human quest for justice.

Cone speaks as a North American black. As he tells us in his autobiography, his earliest experiences were constituted by two realities: white racism and the black church.[10] From white racism he learned of injustice, and from the black church he learned of God's love of justice. Along with other liberation thinkers, he theologizes with a commitment to all who have undergone, and still undergo, experiences of radical injustice. In the Bible, Cone says, we discover a God who inspired the ancient Hebrews to seek liberation from the Egyptians, and who sent Jesus to preach "good news to the poor."[11] It is this same God, he submits, who today inspires people of color to seek freedom from white domination, who inspires women to seek freedom from male domination, and who inspires the poor throughout the world to seek freedom from the domination of the rich.

Those in the First World and elsewhere—often white, male, or affluent—who hear the claims of Cone and other liberation theologians often respond, all too quickly, with questions. Doesn't

God love the oppressor too? Are not they, also, recipients of God's grace? Isn't God, after all, a God of all people?

Cone points out that such questions are often raised with unacknowledged and perhaps unrealized ideological interests in mind. The oppressor asks if God does not love him, too, because he wants to be assured that he is acceptable in spite of the oppressive social practices in which he participates. Liberation theologians are insistent that the God of the oppressed is not one who sanctions the oppressive status quo, or who sanctions those who maintain it. If this is what it means to say that God is a God of all people, then the existence of such a God must be denied.

If, however, the radical nature of the social gospel is not compromised, and if it is realized that radical transformations must occur within society at both a structural and individual level for the sake of justice, then Cone can say that the God of the oppressed is a God of all people.[12] This does not mean that God accepts the dominating practices of the oppressor classes. Rather it means that, in the interests of all people, oppressor and oppressed alike, God seeks an end to oppression. For oppressors and for the oppressed, the love of God is experienced as a call to justice.

Can the God to whom Cone and other liberation theologians point be affirmed by process theology? Can the Whiteheadian understanding of God be helpful in affirming the God of the oppressed? Increasingly, process thinkers suggest that it can. Although most process theologians up to this point have been white, male, and members of the dominant economic class, more and more they have been speaking in solidarity with those who are not. For thinkers such as John Cobb, L. Charles Birch, Schubert Ogden, and Delwin Brown, process theology has itself become a form of liberation theology.[13] In addition, feminist theologians such as Sheila Davaney, Penelope Washbourn, and Marjorie Suchocki are developing perspectives promoting women's liberation in a process context.[14] The argument that emerges from an examination of such thinkers is not that the process perspective mirrors in every aspect the emphases of all liberation perspectives. Indeed it does not; nor could it, since there is, and ought to be, diversity within liberation theologies. Rather the argument is that a distinctive kind of liberation theology can emerge out of process theology: one that emphasizes the relational character of all existence, one that emphasizes ecological sustainability alongside social justice, and one that sees liberation as an ongoing process rather than a settled fact.[15] Amidst these distinctive emphases, a process theology of liberation will indeed affirm, along with Cone and most liberation theologians, that God is a God of the oppressed. It will affirm (1) that God suffers with the poor and oppressed amidst their suffering, and (2) that God is involved in their struggle for liberation. The two natures of the process God—the "consequent" or receptive aspect, and the "primordial" or active aspect—provide a contest for each of these affirmations.

As receptive, the God to whom process thinkers point is one who feels, and empathetically identifies with, each event in the world as it occurs. God is a cosmic consciousness in whose ongoing life the world unfolds, and to whose life new events are continually added. Worldly happenings are felt in such a way that worldly pain becomes divine pain, worldly struggle divine struggle, and worldly joy divine joy. Just as what happens in the body happens in the mind, so what happens in the world happens in God. In this sense Cone is right to say that God is black. The sufferings of black people are God's own sufferings. In addition, God is red, and brown, and female, and male, and young, and old, and animal. Wherever there is suffering and victimization, either of human or nonhuman life, there is God. God is indeed a God of the oppressed.

The active side of God is God's reaction to what is felt. As events in the world occur, they affect God, and God responds by acting in the world. In human life this active response is experienced as an inwardly felt lure, or call, within the depths of prereflective experience. It is a call toward the fullness of life, relative to what is possible and preferable in the circumstances at hand. From moment to moment, this call consists of relevant possibilities for thought, feeling, and action. The possibilities are themselves a stimulus to, and an inspiration for, authentic human creativity. They are changing from circumstance to circumstance, and from person to person, but always they are for individual wholeness and social well-being. At an individual level, they are for wisdom and compassion, not self-deception and hatred of others. At a social level, they are for social justice and ecological sustainability, not injustice and a degradation of nature. Wherever in human life we see a struggle for justice or for sustainability, there we see responsiveness to God. Here, too, Cone is right. God is involved in, and indeed a stimulus for, the struggle for liberation. God is active in the world, again, as a God of the oppressed.

Yet this God of the oppressed, even as involved in the sufferings of the poor and in their struggle for liberation, is also a God who is empty. At least this is the claim that emerges from a process theology that is informed by an encounter with Buddhism. Clearly the suggestion that the God of the oppressed is empty will sound strange to liberation thinkers unacquainted with Buddhist views. It will also sound strange to Buddhists outside the Pure Land tradition who are nontheistic in orientation. Liberation theologians will wonder if the expression is not a denigration of God's significance, and nontheistic Buddhists will wonder if there is a God whose significance can be denigrated. In the following section I will assume, along with Pure Land Buddhists, that there is such a God, one who can well be called Amida. And I will assume, along with liberation theologians, that this God is a God of the oppressed. The task is to understand how this God might be empty.

The Emptiness of God

Already in this chapter I have spoken of emptiness as "the ultimate reality" and God as the "ultimate actuality." Emptiness, I have said, is "that universal and yet nonsubstantial activity, itself expressed as *pratitya samutpada,* of which all sentient beings, God included, are expressions." Clearly this is a distinctive way of understanding emptiness. It is influenced by Whitehead and by contemporary thinkers within the Kyoto School of Japanese Buddhist philosophy.[16] It represents *a* way of understanding emptiness, though not necessarily *the* way, since there is diversity within Buddhism itself on the concept of emptiness. It is a way, I believe, that can be profoundly Buddhist even as it is profoundly Whiteheadian. Let us further analyze it.

To say that emptiness is the ultimate reality is to say that it answers the question of being, or is-ness. If we ask, "What is the being of beings?" or "What is the ultimate 'stuff'—the is-ness—of which all actualities are expressions?" we must answer with the word *emptiness.* Emptiness names two aspects of the fundamental nature of beings, one negative and one positive.

Negatively speaking, emptiness names the fact that all actualities are devoid of "substance" in the Cartesian sense of the word. A substance is something that exists apart from or related to other things and that remains unchanged over time. It is something solid and immutable, self-enclosed and radically independent. If by "thing" we mean a substance of this sort, then there are no things from a Buddhist or Whiteheadian perspective. There is only no-thing-ness, or emptiness.

Yet no-thing-ness is not mere nothingness. Positively speaking, emptiness names the fact that all actualities are constituted by relatedness and pure becoming. Precisely because things are devoid of substance, they are in the depths of their natures open to influence from others and expressive of temporal process. To say the ultimate reality is emptiness, then, is not to say the data of experience are mere illusions. Rather, it is to say that nouns are really verbs, that beings are really becomings, and that these becomings depend on one another for their existence. Actualities are not static facts; they are interdependent processes. In the paradoxical language of Zen, emptiness is fullness.[17]

What, then, is the relationship between emptiness and *pratitya samutpada? Pratitya samutpada,* or dependent origination, is the name that Buddhists give to the fact that all actualities become in dependence on one another. Hence emptiness, as the ultimate reality, is identical with *pratitya samutpada.* This is to say that the fundamental nature of each and every actuality—the ultimate reality of any and every entity—is dependent origination.

For the Buddhist and for process thinkers, there has never been a time when there was not *pratitya samutpada,* and there never will be such a time. Somewhat analogous to the way in which a contemporary physicist can argue that the universe is an infinite series of "big bangs," the Buddhist will suggest that the universe is a beginningless and endless series of interconnected events. Process thinkers will add that the universe is accompanied in its infinite history by God, who, too, is without beginning or end. From a process perspective the history of the universe is that of an infinite series of cosmic epochs, each of which are drawn into those forms of order and growth (physical and in some instances biological, social, and psychological) that are possible in the situations at hand. God—the divine lure—is the one doing the drawing, and in this sense God is the ground of order and growth in the universe. But the drawing itself, which is essential to God's own nature, depends on the existence of other actualities to be drawn. Without a universe of one sort or another, there would be no God; and without God there would be no universe. *Pratitya samutpada* is indeed the ultimate reality, characteristic of God's relation to the world and the world's to God.

Does this belie the traditional Christian claim that God is a creator? For process thinkers, it does not, although divine "creativity" in this case is understood in a unique (though not necessarily unbiblical) way. God's creativity is not that of a single divine fiat that generated the world into existence out of sheer nothingness long ago; rather it is that of a continuous and ongoing process that potentially draws the universe into new forms of actuality relative to what is possible in each situation. The very efficacy of this creativity depends on the creative response of the actualities that are drawn. In their freedom, they may or may not respond to the divine lure. This means that at any given moment what is happening in the universe is the result, not of God's creativity alone, or of the universe's alone, but rather of the joint creativity of God and the universe. Sometimes the historical results of this joint process reflect the world's response to God's lure. In the human arena in the cosmic epoch on the planet earth, for example, achievements of social justice and ecological sustainability on the part of human beings reflect authentic responsiveness to the divine lure. Sometimes, however, the results reveal a divergence from that lure, as the realities of injustice and unsustainability indicate. In both instances, God has been at work, but in the first instance the work has been fulfilled through a sympathetic response on the part of actualities on which God depends, while in the other the work has been frustrated. God's creativity is powerful, but it is not all-determining either in fact or in principle.

Does God know in advance whether or not divine aims will be reciprocated by worldly response? Does God know in advance, for example, whether or not humans will achieve relative justice and sustainability? From a process perspective, the answer is no. God knows what is possible in the future, but not what is actual until it is actual. As events in the world transpire, God becomes aware of them, and they become part of God. The divine aims are themselves adjusted for subsequent events in accordance with what has happened. Both as an actuality who continually shares in the world's destiny and as one who continually adapts aims to fit circumstances, God is in process with the world.

What, then, does it mean to say that God is empty? At least two things. It means (1) that God, like every actuality, is fundamentally dependent on other actualities for God's existence and for the achievement of God's own purposes, and (2) that God, too, is in a process of becoming along with the world. Stated simply, God is an instance of, rather than an exception to, *pratitya samutpada*.

Yet there is a third implication of the idea that God is empty. In Buddhism an understanding of the doctrine of emptiness involves more than a mere establishment of cognitive claims concerning the absence of substantiality and the presence of relationality. It also involves an emotional transformation. To understand that actualities are empty both in the negative and the positive senses of the terms is to understand that actualities are not amenable to personal clinging or egocentric grasping. Because actualities are dependently originating processes rather than static facts, they cannot be held onto as objects of unchanging possession. They can be appreciated and loved in their temporality, but they cannot be owned. One must be free to "let go" of them amidst their temporal transitions and in some cases to "let them be" amidst their unfoldings. To say that God is empty, then, is to say, in addition to the two principles noted above, that (3) even God, amidst God's own unfolding, is unclingable.

Given these three implications of the suggestion that God is empty, we can return to the primary question of the paper. Is it possible or desirable to say that the God of liberation theologies—the God of the oppressed—is also a God who is empty? If this is said, what are its implications for a liberating faith?

The Emptiness of the God of the Oppressed

From what has been said thus far, it should be clear that, if one begins with the metaphysical assumptions of process thought, it is indeed possible to affirm that the God of the oppressed is empty. In this instance "possibility" refers to metaphysical and logical possibility. The point is that one can simultaneously claim that God is a God of the oppressed and that God is empty without being embroiled in a logical contradiction and without violating metaphysical principles. God is the ultimate actuality, and emptiness the ultimate reality.

The more important question is whether such an affirmation would be desirable. Of course, if the affirmation is philosophically valid, as process thinkers believe, then on grounds of sheer truth it is desirable to make the affirmation. Humans have an obligation to acknowledge what is true, and often their lives are enriched in so doing. But I am speaking of a different kind of desirability, that of what is theologically meaningful for those involved in pursuing justice for the disenfranchised. Do Christians who speak from, or in solidarity with, the South having anything to gain by appropriating insights from the East? I suggest that there are at least two things to gain.

First, the Buddhist idea of *pratitya samutpada,* particularly as interpreted in a process context, can offer further support to the liberation idea that God suffers with all that suffer, and that this suffering is part of the divine life. To say that God exemplifies *pratitya samutpada* can be to say that within the depths of God's existence there is an openness to influence from without through which God experiences, and is identified with, the feelings of all who suffer. Of course such an affirmation can also be made from the point of view of substance metaphysics. But often when one says, as one does from a substance perspective, that God simply "chooses" to enter into relations with the world, as if God could do otherwise, the impression is left that the real God—God as changeless and independent—remains behind as a separate agent, somewhat aloof from sufferings of which "he" only distantly partakes. The adoption of a relational metaphysics of the sort one finds in Buddhism and process theology can set the record straight. It can make clear that the fullness of the divine life is by no means aloof. For Christians, it can contribute to an affirmation that the suffering of Jesus on the cross, which has traditionally been understood as an aspect of God's own life, is an expression of, rather than an exception to, what happens anywhere and everywhere. The pain of the world is the pain of God.

The second thing to be gained is more controversial. It concerns the very existence of worldly pain in the first place. I submit that liberation theology has something to gain from Buddhism in dealing with theodicy.

Why, the liberation theologian must inevitably ask, is there so much unnecessary pain in a world that is allegedly loved (at least as the Western tradition has seen it) by an all-powerful God? Why does one child under five die of starvation on the average of every two seconds? Why is at least one woman raped every four seconds? Why is at least one prisoner tortured every eight seconds? Why is at least one dark-skinned person (or in truth why are untold millions of dark-skinned people) denied access to food, clothing, shelter, education, and job opportunities every minute of the day? Why, if God is all-loving and all-powerful, is there so much persistent and pervasive evil?

In dealing with this question, several responses are imaginable. One is to deny that God is all-loving; another is to deny that there is any genuine evil; and still another is to insist that the question is unanswerable. A liberation theology that is influenced by Buddhism—and that therefore sees God as empty—can propose a fourth response. It can affirm that God is all-loving and potentially active in the world as liberator, yet it can deny that God is all-powerful in the classical sense of being all-determining or potentially all-determining. By virtue of *pratitya samutpada,* so the liberation theologian can claim, even God's power is dependent upon worldly response.

Not all liberation theologians would find this fourth alternative attractive. In a different context James Cone, to name a significant example, has forcefully argued that "it is a violation of black faith to weaken either divine love or divine power." Cone rejects the existence of a "finite God." Yet William R. Jones, another black theologian, disagrees with Cone. In *Is God a White Racist?* Jones argues that the notion of an all-loving and all-powerful God is itself inadequate in light of the black experience of suffering.[18] Taking into account racism and other forms of injustice, Jones says, one must inevitably question whether God, if all-powerful, is also all-loving. An all-powerful God who created the world out of nothing, who foresaw from the beginning the forms of unnecessary pain that would result, and who chose then (and chooses now) not to prevent that pain, is less than all-loving. If such a God exists, Jones contends, then this God is a tyrant, a white racist. Against Cone, Jones argues that black theology must turn away from theism of the classical type toward humanism, toward an acknowledgment of the functional ultimacy of humankind.

A liberation theology that is sympathetic to Jones's critique of the classical theodicy, and yet that seeks a theistic rather than a humanistic alternative, may find the idea of God's emptiness helpful. The God who exemplifies *pratitya samutpada* is all-loving in the sense of being affected by oppression and profoundly involved in its remedy, but this God is not all-powerful in the sense of being all-determining or even potentially all-determining. The luring power of this God is that of persuasion rather than coercion, and in order for this power to be fulfilled, the world must itself be persuaded. From a liberation perspective of this sort, even God cannot end racism by fiat. The world must cooperate.

Thus an appropriation of the idea of emptiness on the part of liberation thinkers might serve two interests. It might reinforce and strengthen the idea that the pain of the world is the pain of God. And, as applied to the problem of theodicy, it might enhance an appreciation of God's love for the disenfranchised without holding God indictable for the sufferings that the disenfranchised undergo, and without denying human responsibility for ending the injustices that give rise to such sufferings in the first place.

Of course a liberation theology that appropriates the idea of emptiness in these ways will diverge significantly from many strands of traditional Buddhist thought. Masao Abe has pointed out that much Buddhism has been weak in the area of social justice. By contrast, the theme of justice will be at the center of any liberation theology. And, as Abe has also pointed out, many forms of Buddhism deny the very existence of God and attendant teleological forms of thought. A liberation theology that is Buddhized will nevertheless be theistic and in many respects teleological. Hence liberation theology will be Buddhized in somewhat the same sense that in the past much Western Christianity was Hellenized, or that in the present certain forms of Christian thought and practice are being Africanized or Hispanicized. It will be appropriate a nonbiblical but quite valuable tradition and at the same time transform the tradition that is appropriated.

In addition, of course, a liberation theology that is Buddhized will itself be transformed. For example, whereas liberation perspectives in the past have sometimes invited a solidarity with the oppressed at the expense of a concern for the oppressor, a Buddhized liberation theology will emphasize the welfare of both groups whenever possible. Practically speaking, this means that it will side with those forms of activism and resistance that emphasize nonviolent rather than violent means of social change. And whereas liberation perspectives in the past have often neglected the rights of nature while emphasizing the rights of humans, a Buddhized liberation theology will emphasize the rights of each. It will employ what process theologians call an "ecological" paradigm, in which the interconnectedness and intrinsic value of all forms of life, human and nonhuman, are stressed.

An additional way in which liberation theology might be transformed—along with other forms of Christian theology that are influenced by Buddhism—concerns faith. A Christian faith that has been Buddhized will realize that faith must itself be purged of the view that its object—God as revealed in Christ—is an object on which to cling. It is to the possibility of a nonclinging faith that I turn in the final section.

A Liberating Faith that is Nonclinging

Christian faith is a form of trust in God. It is inspired by Jesus and the earliest witnesses to his life, because in Jesus, so the Christian believes, the trustworthiness of God was shown uniquely and decisively, although not exclusively. Yet Christian faith is not simply a backward-looking focus on the historical Jesus. Faith is also a present-attending and forward-looking affair. It is openness to what the Gospel of John calls the Logos, which is the living spirit of God as immanent within the world. Faith is trust in the Logos as it was revealed in Jesus and other figures from the past, as it exists in the present, and as it can appear in the future.

As directly experienced, this Logos is what I have called the lure of God. It is the continued and yet ever-changing presence of fresh possibilities derived from God for the fullness of life relative to the circumstances at hand. These possibilities are for love and justice, for hope and creativity, for self-affirmation and self-transcendence. They are discovered within, not outside of, the depths of one's immediate experience. Yet they are experienced as given rather than as projected. They are one way in which God is present within each and every human heart.

Nevertheless, the possibilities derived from the Logos may well be items from which a person can hide, perhaps because the person is consumed by other kinds of possibilities. Or they may be possibilities of which a person is aware, but which that person refuses to actualize. It can often seem easier to repeat the patterns of the past, no matter how destructive of one's own well-being, than to respond to that Logos—that wellspring of new possibilities—by which life might be fulfilled for oneself and others. Missing the mark of responding to these possibilities is the essence of sin. Such sin is a mark of almost all human existence to one degree or another and in one way or another. Hence the truth of the doctrine of original sin.

Even when humans fail to respond to the Logos, however, Christians have rightly emphasized that the presence of the Logos continues within each human life. It is always present in the form of immanent possibilities, even if the possibilities remain unactualized because they are ignored or neglected. This continued presence attests to the fact that the Logos is gracious, that is, expressive of divine grace. We find possibilities for newness and hope through the Logos not because we have earned the right to such possibilities, but rather because they are freely given by God. Thus trust in the Logos involves an openness to divine grace.

Within Christianity, another word for the Logos is *Christ.* In this context the word *Christ* refers to more than the historical Jesus. It refers to that beginningless and endless Word of God that became flesh in Jesus, but that was not exhausted by Jesus' life and death. The Logos is the "cosmic Christ" that was revealed in Jesus and with which Jesus was identical. Given this sense of Christ, Christian faith can be defined most clearly as "trust in Christ." It is trust in the Logos, in the universality and potential efficacy of God's Word.

For a Christianity that is open to pluralism—as a Buddhized Christianity would be—trust in Christ may well be discerned among those who do not profess Christianity. Wherever there is an actualization of possibilities for love and justice, for example, there is an openness to the immanence of God, and hence an openness to Christ. This means that the presence of Christ in the world is by no means limited to those who use the word *Christ* or who self-consciously consider themselves Christian. There are those who, in their own way and without conscious reference to Jesus, exhibit an openness to that spirit whom Christians name Christ that Christians can well emulate. From other religions and other traditions, Christians can well discover even deeper dimensions of Christ.

From the perspective of a Christian faith that has been Buddhized, Christ, too, is empty. This means not only that the historical Jesus fully exemplified *pratitya samutpada,* but also that the cosmic Logos is dependently originating. The possibilities derived from God and therein expressive of God's immanence are (1) dependent on the world for their actualization, (2) evolving in their content in relation to the changing circumstances of the world, and (3) unclingable by virtue of their changing character. A faith that is Buddhized is one that is trustful of Christ, but that does not cling to Christ. What can this mean?

To trust Christ is to be open to possibilities derived from God for the fullness of life, appreciative of the fact that they are freely given, committed to their actualization, confident that their presence will continue, and hopeful that their actualization will occur. To trust

Christ without clinging to Christ is to realize that in the interests of life's fullness these possibilities will change from moment to moment, and hence that none can be subjected to static fixation. A nonclinging trust in Christ is one that lets Christ be Christ: dynamic rather than static, evolutionary rather than fixed, flowing rather than rigid, adaptive rather than inflexible. Amidst its commitment to Christ, a nonclinging trust is continuously open to fresh possibilities for creative transformation, cognizant of the fact that it is precisely in the presence of such possibilities that Christ is present. Indeed a nonclinging faith refuses to absolutize any given possibility for creative transformation as final and unsurpassable, because it is aware of the fact that the very essence of Christ is change.

Because liberation theologies are particularly and rightly attentive to possibilities derived from Christ for social justice, a primary temptation of liberation perspectives is to take given possibilities for justice as absolute. These possibilities are usually articulated as visions of a just society toward which all should strive. Particular social and political programs are encouraged as necessary means by which the society that is envisioned is to be realized. Considered in itself, there is nothing wrong—and much that is right—with envisioning a just society in this way and with encouraging concrete ways in which it can be realized. Indeed such envisionment and encouragement can be profoundly responsive to the immanence of God in Christ as relative to particular social situations. What is wrong, at least from a liberation perspective that is Buddhized, is taking any particular vision of a just society, or any given social program, as an absolute.

To take a vision or a program as an absolute is to approach it as if it were incapable of being modified or transformed by changing circumstances and the lure of Christ. A liberation faith that is Buddhized will realize that nothing is incapable of modification or transformation. Even our most dearly held visions of the way the world can be and ought to be, even our most dearly held hopes for social change, can and should be creatively transformed through continued openness to Christ. It is in such openness that the essence of a Buddhized faith will lie. And perhaps it is on such openness, embodied by oppressor and oppressed alike, that the achievement of genuine justice will depend. The only lasting transformations, both at a social level and at an individual level, are those that are ongoing.

NOTES

*This chapter will also be published by the *Journal of Ecumenical Studies* and is used with their permission.

1. John May, "Christian-Buddhist-Marxist Dialogue: A Model for Social Change in Asia?" *Journal of Ecumenical Studies* 19, no. 4 (1982): 737.
2. Ibid.
3. Although in some instances a distinction between liberation theology and political theology may be helpful, I use the phrases interchangeably for purposes of this essay.
4. John B. Cobb, Jr., *Process Theology as Political Theology* (Philadelphia: Westminster Press, 1982); Cobb and L. Charles Birch, *The Liberation of Life* (Cambridge: Cambridge University Press, 1981); Schubert Ogden, *Faith and Freedom: Toward a Theology of Liberation* (Nashville, Tenn.: Abingdon Press, 1979); John B. Cobb, Jr. and W. Widick Schroeder, ed., *Process Philosophy and Social Thought* (Chicago: Center for the Scientific Study of Religion, 1981); Sheila Davaney, ed., *Feminism and Process Thought* (New York and Toronto: Edwin Mellen Press, 1981); Delwin Brown, *To Set at Liberty: Toward a Theology of Liberation* (Maryknoll, NY: Orbis, 1980).
5. See the interview of Cobb and Abe in *Buddhist-Christian Studies* 1, (1981). See also Cobb, *Beyond Dialogue: Toward a Mutual Transformation of Christianity and Buddhism* (Philadelphia: Fortress Press, 1982), 110–14, and Cobb, "Buddhist Emptiness and the Christian God," *Journal of the American Academy of Religion* (March 1977).
6. Alfred North Whitehead, *Process and Reality,* corrected edition, eds. David Ray Griffin and Donald W. Sherburne (New York: Free Press, 1978), 7, 20, 88, 225.
7. The fact that from a biblical perspective God's creativity is creation out of chaos rather than creation out of nothing is discussed and amplified by David Ray Griffin "Creation Out of Chaos and the Problem of Evil," in *Encountering Evil: Live Options in Theodicy,* ed. Stephen T. Davis (Atlanta: John Knox Press, 1981), 101–18. See also Griffin's *God, Power, and Evil: A Process Theodicy* (Philadelphia: Westminster Press, 1976).
8. See Cobb, *Beyond Dialogue,* 128–36.
9. James H. Cone, *God of the Oppressed* (New York: Seabury Press, 1975), *passim.*
10. James H. Cone, *My Soul Looks Back* (Nashville, Tenn.: Abingdon, 1982).
11. Luke 4:18–19.
12. Much more emphatic on this point than Cone is the black theologian, J. Deotis Roberts. See Roberts, *Liberation and Reconciliation: A Black Theology* (Philadelphia: Westminster Press, 1971). Cone is in disagreement with Roberts on the centrality of reconciliation. See Cone, *God of the Oppressed,* 239. Nevertheless I understand both Cone and Roberts to be affirming the universality of divine love.

13. See note 2.

14. See Davaney, *Feminism and Process Thought*. See also Marjorie Suchocki, *God–Christ–Church: A Practical Guide to Process Theology* (New York: Crossroad Publishing Co., 1982).

15. See Birch and Cobb, *The Liberation of Life,* for a strong emphasis on ecological sustainability. See also Cobb, *Process Theology as Political Theology,* 111–33.

16. For an anthology of essays written by thinkers of the Kyoto School, see Frederick Franck, *The Buddha Eye: An Anthology of the Kyoto School* (New York: Crossroad Publishing Co., 1982).

17. For an excellent discussion of the concept of emptiness in Buddhism, see Frederick Streng, *Emptiness: A Study in Religious Meaning* (Nashville: Abingdon, 1967).

18. William R. Jones, *Is God a White Racist?* (New York: Doubleday, 1973).

Contributors

GORDON L. ANDERSON, Ph.D. candidate, Department of Religion, Claremont Graduate School, California; Executive Director, Professors World Peace Academy, New York, New York

PAUL BOUVIER, United Nations Delegate in Geneva for Caritas Internationalis, Geneva, Switzerland

RITA NAKASHIMA BROCK, Instructor of Philosophy and Religion, Stephens College, Columbia, Missouri

KATHLEEN DUGAN, Associate Professor, Religious Studies, University of San Diego, Alcala Park, San Diego, California

FREDERICK FERRÉ, Professor of Philosophy and Head, Department of Philosophy, University of Georgia, Athens, Georgia

DAYA KRISHNA, Professor and Head, Department of Philosophy, University of Rajasthan, Jaipur, India

RITA H. MATARAGNON, Chairperson and Associate Professor, Department of Psychology, Ateneo de Manila University, Manila, Philippines; Population Council post-doctoral fellow in population psychology at the University of North Carolina, Chapel Hill, North Carolina

JAY B. McDANIEL, Assistant Professor, Department of Religion, Hendrix College, Conway, Arkansas

JERRY ITUMELENG MOSALA, Lecturer, Department of Religious Studies, University of Cape Town, Cape Town, South Africa

ELLEN H. PALANCA, Associate Professor, Department of Economics, Ateneo de Manila University, Manila, Philippines

HANS SCHWARZ, Professor of Systematic Theology and Contemporary Theological Issues, University of Regensburg, Regensburg, West Germany

HAROLD W. TURNER, Director, Study Centre for New Religious Movements in Primal Societies, Selly Oak Colleges, Birmingham University, Birmingham, United Kingdom

INDEX

Index

Index